S0-EKM-663

WORDS OF TRAINING
FOR THE NEW WAY

Witness Lee

VOLUME TWO

Living Stream Ministry
Anaheim, California

© 1988 Witness Lee

First Edition, 6,250 copies. December 1988.

ISBN 0-87083-407-X (hardcover)
ISBN 0-87083-427-4 (softcover)

Published by

Living Stream Ministry
1853 W. Ball Road, Anaheim, CA 92804 U.S.A.
P. O. Box 2121, Anaheim, CA 92814 U.S.A.

Printed in the United States of America

CONTENTS

PREFACE

This volume is a translation from the Chinese of messages given in Taipei, Taiwan, by Brother Witness Lee in 1987. These messages were given during the months of October, November, and December to trainees participating in the Full-time Training in Taipei, Taiwan.

CHAPTER THIRTEEN

THE STEPS TO LEAD PEOPLE IN THE NEW WAY

(1)

Scripture Reading: Acts 4:8; 13:9; 2 Cor. 4:13; Rom. 10:12-13; 2 Tim. 2:22; 2 Cor. 3:17; 1 Cor. 14:26; Heb. 10:25; Rom. 10:9; Eph. 5:18-19; Col. 3:16

PREACHING THE GOSPEL BY HOME VISITATION— THE FOUNDATION ESTABLISHED BY GOD IN THE BIBLE

In the last three years, I have been speaking on the new way. The purpose of that speaking was to have a complete rearrangement according to the Bible in the ways of meeting and service which we have had for the past sixty years. I have said before that the big meetings and the small meetings are like the two wings of an airplane; you cannot afford to lose either one. I have also said before that the lack of results in our gospel preaching in the past years, in spite of our labor and diligence, was due to a problem in the way of doing things. If the way of doing things is not effective, then naturally the efficiency will be reduced. We have now found out that the most scriptural and effective way of preaching the gospel is to visit people in their homes. This was determined based on the revelation and pattern seen in the Bible, our study of the gospel preaching methods adopted by the various groups in Christianity in the last two thousand years, and our own history for the past sixty years. This was the foundation established by God in the Bible.

After Adam fell, God did not call him while He was sitting in the heavens; rather, He came to the earth to seek him, and said to him, "Where art thou?" (Gen. 3:9). Later, when God wanted to bring His grace to His chosen people, He again did not call man while He was sitting in the heavens; He came to the earth Himself to become flesh, to become a man. While He was on the earth, He Himself went to visit sinners from place to place. He went even to that cursed city of Jericho to visit a great sinner called Zaccheus, and said to him, "Today I must stay in your house." Then He said, "Today salvation has come to this house" (Luke 19:5, 9). The Lord also went to Samaria, a place despised and rejected by the Jews, to visit an immoral woman (John 4:3-4).

When the Lord was carrying out the gospel work on the earth, He did not ask His disciples to go to different places to hold gospel conventions so that He could save thousands of people by simply sounding a call. Instead, the Lord sent His disciples to go out. First, He sent the twelve apostles (Luke 9:1-2); then He sent the seventy disciples. He asked them to go to city after city and home after home to seek out the sons of peace (Luke 10:1, 6). The Lord did not send those who had doctoral degrees, who had positions, and who were capable, to draw people. Rather, He sent those unknown disciples, two by two, to go out to visit people in their homes. Therefore, our going out today to visit people's homes to preach the gospel to them, to get them saved and baptized, is something absolutely according to the example set up by the Lord in the Bible.

From a human viewpoint, it is not an easy thing to go out to knock on people's doors. If you were to invite your friends to attend a big gospel meeting where they could sit inside a grandly built chapel with a stately atmosphere, a piano and other musical instruments, a choir, and a famous speaker preaching, you would feel honored. But concerning the matter of visiting people's homes to preach the gospel, even the brothers, not to mention the sisters, would feel awkward knocking on people's doors. They are afraid that after the door is opened, they may be rebuked by people. I stayed before in Shanghai where the door from one house to the next was not more than ten feet away, yet the neighbors would not care for one another. If you were to knock on doors to preach the gospel, nine out of ten times you would encounter rebuke. It is not easy to knock on doors in Hong Kong either, and it is even more difficult in northern Europe.

Preaching the gospel by knocking on doors requires you to be prepared to experience hardship, to look at people's long faces, and even to suffer rebuke from others, yet still to smile at them. This is indeed not an easy matter. This is the reason that this matter of preaching the gospel by visiting people's homes is not adopted by many Christians even though it is emphatically revealed and testified in the Bible. This way requires us to pay a considerable price, yet human beings would rather avoid the hardship and take the easy way. Today in the Lord's recovery, if we want the Lord to have a way in the matter of gospel preaching, we must follow this example of the Lord who was incarnated and humbled to visit people, and go to visit people's homes to bring the gospel to them. This is the most effective way to preach the gospel.

ONE-FOURTH PREACHING THE GOSPEL
BY HOME VISITATION AND
THREE-FOURTHS SUPPORTING AND SUPPLYING

We should not think that everyone in the church can go out to visit people for preaching the gospel. We only expect that among one hundred meeting attendants, there will be twenty-five who can go out. These should go out to knock on doors every other week. They should go out two times a month, twenty-four times a year. Every year each person can definitely bring eight persons to be saved. By this way, twenty-five persons can bring in two hundred new ones. These twenty-five will then bring with them another twenty-five, totaling fifty persons, to lead those two hundred newly baptized ones to regularly have home meetings and attend small group meetings that they may enter into the church life. In this way, we hope that within one year there will be one hundred new ones remaining in the church life. Therefore, we do not need everyone to go out to knock on doors; if there are one-fourth doing it, that will be adequate. The remaining three-fourths that stay behind need to support and supply them.

HOME MEETINGS, GROUP MEETINGS, AND DISTRICT MEETINGS

After we have visited people's homes and helped them to believe and be baptized to be saved, we must lead them to begin having home meetings in their homes. These home meetings will help them to know the Lord's salvation and other truths concerning a new believer's living. It is best to have this kind of home meeting once a week. The meeting time should not be too short. In every meeting, the new believers should be brought into a particular item of spiritual knowledge. Besides this, we should lead them to attend the neighboring group meetings so that they can know and have fellowship with other believers for the mutual care of one another. After a few months, we should bring them to the bigger district meetings; sometimes, according to the need, we may even bring them to the corporate meeting of the whole church. Some have misunderstood that we do not need big meetings. This is not accurate.

I hope that all the trainees, the elders from different localities, and all the serving ones can understand the new way that we have seen. When you go to different places to speak of these things, you have to speak clearly. You should not give people the impression that we want every saint to go out to knock on doors, and if they do not, they will be treated differently and marked out as opposing or disagreeing ones. We surely believe that visiting people by knocking on doors is the best and most effective way to preach the gospel, but we still have to consider the situation of the church and lead the saints according to their practical conditions. When all of you go to different places to fellowship about the new way, you should not have prejudice, nor should you fail to mention anything; you should speak accurately and completely so that a complete picture will be presented. Only in this way can misunderstanding and even unnecessary opposition be avoided. The new way is altogether a biblical way; there is indeed no ground for any opposition.

THE STEPS FOR LEADING PEOPLE IN THE NEW WAY

Being Filled with the Spirit and
Speaking by Faith to Preach the Gospel

The first step in preaching the gospel, having meetings, and carrying out the service in the new way is to be filled with the Spirit inwardly and outwardly. In the Bible, the words used for inward filling and outward filling are different. In Chinese we make a distinction between the two. In order to participate in the church life, gospel activities, and all the services, the primary thing needed is to be filled with the Spirit within and without. Therefore, when we go out to knock on doors, we have to confess our sins thoroughly and pray so that we can obtain the filling of the Spirit.

After we are filled with the Spirit, we have to speak by faith. In 2 Corinthians 4:13, this faith is termed the "spirit of faith." It is spirit, as well as faith. We exercise such a spirit to believe and speak the things we have experienced of the Lord. Every time we go out to visit people to preach the gospel, we must go by this faith. We believe that when we go out to knock on doors, it is the Triune God who brings us with Him to knock on doors. Moreover, when people are willing to open their doors to us, it is God who asks them to open the door. Therefore we speak by the Triune God. This is our gospel preaching in the new way, full of spirit and full of faith, speaking by the spirit and also by faith. If we are this kind of person, spontaneously we will be able to help the newly saved ones, leading them to be filled with the Spirit inwardly and outwardly, so that they will be able to speak and preach the gospel by faith with boldness and testify to their relatives, friends, and neighbors. This is the first step in our leading people in the new way.

Leading People to Call on the Name
of the Lord Spirit

The second step in leading people in the new way is to lead them to call on the name of the Lord Spirit. We do not only call on the name of the Lord, but also call on the name of the Lord Spirit. Now our Lord is the Lord Spirit; He is the Spirit (2 Cor. 3:17-18). The Spirit is invisible, untouchable, yet we can sense Him. The name of this Lord Spirit is Jesus. When we call on the Lord Jesus, we are calling on this Lord Spirit. When you go to lead people, you need to present this clearly. You have to tell people, "Our God is the Savior Jesus Christ. He is the living Spirit today. While I am speaking with you, He is here. Furthermore, I am speaking with you by this Spirit. This Spirit is now in your mouth. Therefore you have to open up your mouth and call on the name of the Lord Jesus from deep within." Then you have to help him to call accurately. This is like installing light bulbs. After everything is installed and connected, all you need to do is turn on the electricity and the light bulbs will shine. When a person calls on the Lord, he should not merely call from the throat, nor should he merely call with a sincere heart; he must call from the depth of his being, that is, from his spirit. In this way, he is joined to the Lord, the Spirit. When we go to help the newly saved ones, we need to lead them to call on the name of the Lord who is the Spirit, since this was how they were saved in the beginning.

The Apostle Paul wrote an Epistle to Timothy. At that time Timothy had already become Paul's co-worker. Paul charged Timothy by asking him to "pursue...with those who call on the Lord out of a pure heart" (2 Tim. 2:22). This implies that our whole life should be a life of calling on the Lord. We call on the Lord in the morning; we call on the Lord also in the evening. Our daily life is a life of calling on the Lord. This is not a form but a living. Whenever we call, we touch the Lord within who is the Spirit, and get the supply. You need to lead the new ones to read Romans 10:12-13, that they may see that God is so rich and that they need to call on the name of the Lord in order to obtain these riches. We have to lead people to establish a life of calling on the name of the Lord as soon as they are saved.

Leading People
to Realize the Meetings of the Believers
Being Mutual

The third step in leading people in the new way is to lead the new ones to realize that the meetings of the believers are mutual. Christianity has already brought people to an erroneous situation, that whenever the services of Christianity are mentioned, people immediately have the concept of going to a chapel and listening to the preaching of a father, a pastor, or a preacher. That practice is one-sided, not mutual. But 1 Corinthians 14:26 says that when the whole church comes together, "each one has a psalm, has a teaching, has a revelation, has a tongue, has an interpretation." This clearly shows us that the believers' meetings are mutual. You speak and I listen; I speak and you listen. Everyone speaks and everyone listens. We speak to one another and listen to one another. This is the believers' meeting as revealed in the Bible.

Also Hebrews 10:25 says, "Not forsaking the assembling of ourselves together,...but exhorting one another." From this you can see that the Christian meetings are full of exhorting one another and teaching one another. Even the brothers and sisters who have been in the church for a few decades are not clear concerning this kind of proper meeting. Therefore as soon as we start to change the system, the original habit of meeting becomes a problem. In principle, the changing of the system is not a matter of big meetings or small meetings, but a matter of whether one person is speaking with the rest listening, or whether everyone is speaking with everyone listening. It does not mean that if you change the big meetings to small meetings that you have succeeded. Rather, you have to change the habit of one person speaking with the rest listening to everyone speaking and everyone listening.

Up to today, this habit is still not thoroughly removed. In the concept of most of the brothers and sisters, the meetings are for listening to messages and not for speaking. I am afraid that even you who are sitting here, in your subconscious mind, also desire to attend a big meeting with one person speaking and the rest listening. Therefore, it is really difficult to change the system. This is because on the one hand, the habit built up through the many years is not easily changed; and on the other hand, the practice of one person speaking with the rest listening is easily achieved, while that of everyone speaking is not. This kind of meeting in mutuality demands everyone to be prepared. You can no longer be as before—not being watchful, not praying, not preparing the spirit, not exercising faith, and feeling that it was adequate as long as you came to the meeting. Now the new way demands us to be watchful, to live in the spirit, to exercise the spirit, and to speak by the spirit. In this way, when we come to the meetings, we will be able to speak for the Lord. Also, we will be restrained in our speaking, not taking up all the time but allowing others to carry on the speaking. This kind of meeting in mutuality will be fresh and living and full of supply.

I hope that you can pick up this burden of everyone going to the meeting to speak the Lord's word and leading the newly saved ones to speak the Lord's word. As soon as a person is saved, you should immediately set up a meeting in his home and lead him to speak, so that he can realize that the believers' meetings are mutual and are not like the situation in the chapels of Christianity. After two or three months, you should bring him to the group meeting formed by a number of the neighboring families and also have him practice speaking in that meeting. Gradually a number of these groups can come together to form a bigger district meeting. In this way, after they have become stable and have attained to a certain level of practice in speaking the Lord's word, you can further bring them to the big meetings so they will know that there are big meetings as well as small meetings in the church. It does not matter whether it is a small meeting or a big meeting, the principle is to speak to one another and listen to one another, and not to have one person speaking and the rest listening.

BELIEVERS' MEETINGS BEING FOR SPEAKING FOR THE LORD AND LISTENING TO OTHERS SPEAKING FOR THE LORD

The fourth step in leading people in the new way is to lead the new ones to understand that the church meetings are for the believers to speak for the Lord and to listen to others speaking for the Lord. First, you can speak by the words in the Bible. Any page from Genesis to Revelation can be used for speaking. Besides that, you can also speak by means of the hymns. Every hymn in our hymnal is a message, full of words of revelation. They are a very good means for us to speak for the Lord. Both Ephesians 5 and Colossians 3 mention that we have to use psalms, hymns, and spiritual songs to speak to one another, admonish one another, and also sing and psalm to the Lord. This shows us that the hymns are first for speaking, then for singing. Third, you can also speak by means of spiritual publications. We have many spiritual publications among us such as *Life Lessons*, *Truth Lessons*, and Life-study Messages. All of these can be used as materials for our speaking. As long as we practice in these areas during our daily living, we will have something to speak when we come to the meetings.

In the regular meetings of the church, there is no need of a definite topic, nor the need to be tied down by a topic. The topic is left in the hands of the Holy Spirit. If every one of the brothers and sisters would speak when coming together, the items touched will definitely be very rich, and there will be no need to set a specific topic. This kind of meeting with speaking to one another and listening to one another should be as frequent as twice a week. When everyone comes together, we do not talk about news or stories, but speak about the Bible, hymns, and the spiritual publications among us. In this way, the meeting will definitely be living and rich. I hope that these words are an explanation of the new way, so that everyone can understand the commission the Lord has given us and the goal toward which we should press.

A message given by Brother Witness Lee in Taipei on October 27, 1987.

CHAPTER FOURTEEN

THE STEPS TO LEAD PEOPLE IN THE NEW WAY

(2)

Scripture Reading: Acts 4:8; 13:9; 2 Cor. 4:13; Rom. 10:12-13; 2 Tim. 2:22; 2 Cor. 3:17; 1 Cor. 14:26; Heb. 10:25; Rom. 10:9; Eph. 5:18-19; Col. 3:16

The most crucial step to lead people in the new way is the step of meeting. How should we meet? In the last two thousand years, this has been a matter every seeker of the Lord has been concerned about, and this has also been a big problem that all the denominations of Christianity faced when they were first established.

THE BELIEVERS' MEETINGS NEEDING TO COMPLETELY FOLLOW THE REVELATION AND PATTERN IN THE NEW TESTAMENT

Concerning the believers' meetings, we may take some of the Old Testament principles as reference, but we cannot follow the Old Testament in details, otherwise, we will be trapped in dead letters. Therefore, concerning the matter of meetings, we must completely follow the revelation and pattern in the New Testament.

Among the four Gospels at the beginning of the New Testament, only the Gospel of John mentions the matter of worship. Chapter four records the conversation between the Lord and a sinful, immoral woman. When the Lord Jesus asked her concerning her husband, she changed the topic to the matter of worship, attempting to cover up her immoral and sinful history. At that time, the Lord Jesus told her that the worship of God was not on the mountain in Samaria, nor in Jerusalem, but in the human spirit (vv. 21, 23). We ought to believe that when the Lord Jesus was speaking with her, He brought her into the true worship. The true worship of the believers is to contact God the Spirit with the human spirit (v. 24). This is also to drink the Lord as the living water. This is the worship of God mentioned in the Gospels.

In Acts, we cannot find the term "worship services." Although sometimes the disciples went to the temple, that referred to the services of the Jewish people according to the Old Testament and not to the meetings of the New Testament believers. In the Epistles, the term "worship services" is not used, but rather "meetings" or "gatherings" is used. In Revelation, there is no mention of worship services at all; instead, it mentions numerous times the matter of eating. Chapter two verse 7 says, "To him who overcomes, to him I will give to eat of the tree of life, which is in the paradise of God." Verse 17 says, "To him who overcomes, to him I will give of the hidden manna." Chapter three verse 20 says, "If anyone hears My voice and opens the door, I will come in to him and dine with him and he with Me." Chapter twenty-two verse 17 says, "He who wills, let him take the water of life freely." This eating and drinking is the worship that God wants in the New Testament.

ATTENDING WORSHIP SERVICES
NOT BEING IN THE NEW TESTAMENT

Today there is a big mountain standing before us. This is the worship service established by Satan in the past two thousand years through degraded Christianity. This has become a great hindrance to us in the Lord's recovery who desire to meet according to God's New Testament economy. The concept of attending worship services has already been deeply rooted within people. Once a person has repented and believed in the Lord Jesus, he immediately has a reaction within himself saying, "I have to find a chapel to attend services." I believe that when you go to the community to lead newly saved ones to have home meetings, you will encounter some asking the same type of question, "Where do you go for worship services?" They think within their heart that since they are Christians, they should join a certain church. The best would be one which has a good reputation, is proper, and has a decent chapel with a solemn atmosphere so that upon entering, people will pay great respect. This kind of concept is already deeply rooted within most people, even ourselves. Subconsciously we would rather have a beautiful meeting hall with believers filing in each Lord's Day morning, being seated in an orderly manner, and waiting quietly for the responsible brothers to call the hymns to begin the meeting. But what is revealed in the Bible is not like this. First Corinthians 14:26 says, "Whenever you come together, each one has a psalm, has a teaching, has a revelation, has a tongue, has an interpretation." The phrase "each one has" nullifies the matter of attending the worship services of Christianity. Therefore, in talking about the steps to lead people in the new way, we must first understand that attending worship services is absolutely not of God. In the New Testament there is not such a thing as attending worship services.

THE TRUE WORSHIP OF GOD IN THE NEW TESTAMENT

Now I want to show you a portrait of the true worship of God in the New Testament so that you may have a clear vision. When the Lord Jesus was thirty years old, He came out to fulfill His ministry for God. He went back and forth between Galilee and Judea leading people to know God. In those three and a half years, the Jews were there worshipping God in the temple in Jerusalem as usual in an orderly manner according to the rituals and regulations of the Old Testament. Yet the Lord Jesus had nothing to do with their worship. Although sometimes He went to the temple in Jerusalem, He did not go to attend the services of the Jews. Rather, when everyone came together for worship, He took a whip of cords to cast out all those who were buying and selling in the temple and He overturned the tables of the money-changers and the seats of those who were selling the doves (Matt. 21:12). Those who were buying and selling in the temple were related to the worship of God, but the Lord Jesus cast them out one by one. This shows us clearly that He was outside of the worship in the temple.

Suppose you were there at that time. Would you be following Jesus the Nazarene to know God, or would you be going to the temple of Judaism to worship God? I do not believe that any among the ones seated here could break the traditional concept, would cease going to the orthodox temple to worship God, but instead, would follow Jesus to know God, and even would follow Jesus to the temple to cast out those buying and selling with a whip. I am afraid that you might instead condemn the Lord Jesus for going to the place of worship to disturb the order for worshipping God. However, you have to realize that in those three and a half years, God was not in the temple in Jerusalem to be worshipped, but was following Jesus, and was with Jesus, to be worshipped by man.

In the three and a half years of His work on the earth, the Lord did not go to attend any church services; He did not even have any sequence or order to His work; He seemed to be at ease under any circumstance. When the disciples went into the boat, He also went into the boat. When the boat was near the shore, and the disciples left the boat, He also left the boat. When He saw someone possessed by demons, He went to cast them out. When He knew people were trying to force Him to be king, He stayed away from them. There was a time when many were following Him, and after having been with Him for three days in the wilderness with nothing to eat, He was moved with compassion, and performed a miracle. He used seven loaves and a few fishes to feed them (Matt. 15:32-37). On another occasion, the disciples were in a boat crossing over the sea at night, and due to the contrary winds the boat was under attack by the waves. Suddenly Jesus was walking on the sea toward them. The disciples thought it was a phantom and cried out. "But immediately Jesus spoke to them, saying, Have courage; It is I; do not fear. And Peter answered Him and said, Lord, if it is You, command me to come to You on the waters. And He said, Come. And Peter, coming down from the boat, walked on the waters and came toward Jesus. But seeing the strong wind, he was afraid; and beginning to sink, he cried out, saying, Lord, save me! And immediately Jesus stretched out His hand and took hold of him.... And when they went up into the boat, the wind ceased. And those who were in the boat worshipped Him, saying, Truly You are the Son of God" (Matt. 14:24-33). Do you know that this is the worship to God? The genuine worship to God is to have His presence. It does not matter whether you are in the wilderness, at the seashore, or on the sea. As long as you have the presence of God, and you enjoy Him and He enjoys you, that is the genuine worship. This Jesus Christ is just God Himself. He was the very God whom the Jews were trying to worship in the temple, but He was not there with them. In the temple they only had the name of God in vain, void of His presence. The presence of God was with the walking on the waves; the presence of God was with the distribution of bread and fish to the multitude in the wilderness. If you were in that situation, you were in the presence of God. In that situation, God came to give Himself to be received and enjoyed by men. We should receive and enjoy Him in His presence that He may be happy and that we may be satisfied. This is the best worship in the universe.

NEEDING TO HAVE A THOROUGH CHANGE IN OUR CONCEPT OF MEETING

I hope that your concept can be thoroughly changed so that you no longer would appreciate the traditional things of Christianity such as the magnificent chapels and the sermons given by famous preachers. We have to remove completely from our midst the habit of attending worship services. I studied the Bible over and over again, but I could not find any record of attending worship services. Instead, I found that the church in the home is mentioned a number of times (Rom. 16:5; 1 Cor. 16:19; Col. 4:15; Philem. 2). This shows us that the primary meeting place of the church in the early days was the homes of the saints. That kind of meeting had neither regulations nor the need of rituals. I hope that our home meetings will have no restrictions; people can even sit on the floor. Some may feel that this way is too disorderly and that it makes it difficult to bring people to be saved. The bankers, general managers, professors, doctors, and those with money and position may not be willing to come. That is correct. There may be some not willing to come, but those who are willing to come are not few. Actually, there are not that many who are rich and have position; rather, most are ordinary people. Paul in 1 Corinthians 1 says, "For you see your calling, brothers, that there are not many wise according to flesh, not many powerful, not many wellborn. But God has chosen the foolish of the world...and God has chosen the weak of the world...and the lowborn of the world and the despised...things which are not...." (vv. 26-28). At any rate, we have to change our concept toward meeting. The way of meeting as revealed in the New Testament is absolutely not like that being practiced by Christianity today.

By God's mercy, I will boast a little. Through over sixty years of effort, I may say that I have studied the Bible thoroughly. In the United States, I spent twelve years to write footnotes in English for every one of the twenty-seven books of the New Testament. I have studied dozens of the reference books in Christianity such as the most authoritative translations of the Bible, dictionaries, word studies, and concordances. Sometimes, just to write one footnote, I spent over a week's time and searched through nearly all the reference books. I have also spent time to study the history of Christianity; I have thoroughly studied the practices and beliefs of various groups and denominations in Christianity in the western world. I say all this to you so that you will know that the decision we made three years ago to change the system was not a light matter. I have had over fifty years of experience in working for the Lord. I traveled through many places during twenty years in mainland China. After I went to Taiwan, I traveled back and forth for a period of ten years between Taiwan and Southeast Asia. Then I went to the United States where for twenty-six years, I saw, heard, observed, and studied from coast to coast and from the north to the south. Therefore, I have great assurance concerning the matter of changing the system. We have to push out from our midst this high mountain of attending church services. Then we can be delivered, and the Lord will have a way.

Some have said that the change of system which I have been speaking about for the last three years is scriptural in every respect, but they do not believe that the change of system can succeed. Brothers, can the Lord's word not be fulfilled? Because it has not been fulfilled in the last two thousand years, does this mean that it will never be fulfilled? I believe that the heavens and earth will pass away, but every iota and every tittle of the word spoken by the Lord will be fulfilled. Sooner or later the Lord will have to clear the path and fulfill His own word. May every one of us by faith declare that this way will be successful! If it is not yet successful today, tomorrow it will be successful; if it is not successful with us, it will be successful with others.

THE STEPS TO LEAD PEOPLE IN THE NEW WAY

Leading People to Know the Lord Jesus as the Spirit and to Call upon His Name

Now I want to continue talking about the steps to lead people in the new way. First, you need to lead people to know the Lord Jesus as the Spirit and to call upon His name. When you go out to visit people to preach the gospel, right after getting them saved or in the next visit, you need to lead them to know this Jesus in whom we have believed. When He was on the cross, He was our Savior; now in resurrection He has become a life-giving Spirit to enter into our spirit to be the Spirit of life within us. Therefore, we have to lead the newly saved ones to call on the Lord Jesus from deep within. Upon waking up every morning, they should begin calling on the Lord Jesus. Then, in their daily life, in whatever they are doing, they would continue calling while they are working. This kind of calling on the Lord is like deep breathing which definitely makes us feel very comfortable within.

Leading People to Confess Their Sins
in Order to Be Filled with the Holy Spirit

Second, you need to lead people to confess their sins that they may be filled with the Holy Spirit. We have to lead people to realize that the Spirit of the Lord Jesus cannot tolerate sins. Wherever He is, no sins are allowed. Therefore, we have to lead the new ones to confess their sins; the more they do it and the more thoroughly they do it, the better it is. They need to confess their sins every day even when they do not feel sinful. The more they confess, the more sins they will realize; the more sins they realize, the more they will confess. Eventually they will be filled and taken over within by the Lord.

Leading People to Learn to Speak the Lord

Third, you need to lead people to learn to speak the Lord. They should first learn to confess the Lord's name. After they know how to say "Jesus Christ," they can add a few more words like "Jesus Christ is my Savior." Then, a few more words can be added, "Jesus Christ is my Savior. This Savior today is the Spirit, and He lives in me to be my life." This is like a little child learning to speak. Every word is taught by the mother. The mother teaches him every day, and he listens every day. Gradually, he will understand the meaning of the words and will know how to speak. We need to teach the newly saved ones to speak the Lord's word just as the parents teach their children.

We can also lead people to learn to speak the Lord by the words of the Bible. The Chinese Recovery Version of the New Testament will soon be available. I hope that it can be in each one's hand. This will definitely be a great help to our learning to speak the Lord. Besides, we can also speak the Lord by means of the hymns. We must realize that the hymns are primarily for speaking, not for singing (Eph. 5:19; Col. 3:16). In our practice of speaking the Lord's word, the more we speak, the more we are filled with the Spirit. Eventually, there will be a river of living water flowing out of us unceasingly. This is just like what one hymn says, "The Spirit begets the spirit, the spirit worships the Spirit, until I am filled with the Spirit. The Spirit has become the word, full of the riches of life, flowing out rivers of living water" (Chinese *Hymns* #450). I hope that the brothers and sisters in the Lord's recovery, as well as the newly saved ones under their leading, will be able to speak the Lord. As soon as they open their mouths, they should be able to speak without ceasing so that thousands of people may believe in the Lord and be saved.

THE NEW WAY REQUIRING US TO BE OVERCOMERS

Now I would entreat you, whether or not you agree with the change of system, to accept the fact that the old system is not fruitful. Formerly, for over thirty years we have been in the old system, and the number of people has not increased much, nor the number of churches. The brothers and sisters all loved the Lord and fervently gave themselves, but their service has not had much effect, and the meetings have not had much influence on people. Today the Lord is leading us to take the new way. This requires every one of us to be an overcomer in our daily life and to bear fruit in order to arrive at the increase and spread of the church.

To be an overcomer is not as difficult as you formerly thought. As long as you are saved through calling on the name of the Lord Spirit, and you know that this Lord is now the Spirit, He will live within you. When you commit sins, you must confess your sins and allow His blood to cleanse your sins daily; in this way there will be no barriers between you and Him at any time, and you will walk according to the Spirit. Then you will be an overcomer. Romans is a book on the Christian life, and it emphasizes our walking according to the Spirit (8:4). Are you angry? Are you going to lose your temper? Try simply walking according to the Spirit. If the Spirit is not angry, you will not be angry either. If the Spirit does not lose His temper, you will not lose your temper either. What the Spirit does not do, you will not do either. This is to walk according to the Spirit.

Romans 12:11 says, "Burning in spirit, serving the Lord as a slave." If you would walk according to the Spirit in every matter, then your spirit will be burning from morning until evening. This is an overcomer. Once your spirit is burning, you will definitely speak the Lord's word unceasingly. The more you speak, the more you have to speak, and you will keep speaking. You will speak at home, and you will also speak in the group meeting; you will speak in the neighbors' home, and you will also speak on the bus. If you speak unceasingly in your daily life, you will be an overcomer. Since what is within will be manifested without, this kind of person will spontaneously be full of the Lord's word when he comes to the meeting.

NOT NEEDING A DEFINITE TOPIC IN THE MEETING

I feel that in the various meetings of the church, there is no need of definite topics. Formerly with one person speaking and the rest listening, one week the speaker might speak on justification, and another week he might speak on sanctification. When he speaks on justification, he may not necessarily have the reality of being justified; when he speaks on sanctification, he may not necessarily have a sanctified living. Now, we may not be speaking on justification or sanctification, but if we are calling on the Lord's name every day, walking according to the Spirit, burning in spirit, and speaking the Lord's word to people, this is the justified behavior and the sanctified living. When we come together, you speak, I speak, and everyone speaks the Lord's word. Then the meetings will be living, and the church will also be living. This is the way the Lord wants to take today.

A message given by Brother Witness Lee in Taipei on October 29, 1987.

CHAPTER FIFTEEN

THE INCLUSIVENESS OF THE NEW WAY

(1)

This morning I want to fellowship with you concerning the inclusiveness of the new way. This has been the burden within me for a long time. From the first day I mentioned the need to change the system and take the new way, I heard that a very small number of saints among us had different opinions, especially after we had the gospel preaching by visiting people. From that time, I was prepared to find an opportunity to present to everyone a complete picture of the inclusiveness of the new way in its entirety.

THE NEED TO PRACTICE THE NEW WAY

We already tried this new way over fifty years ago, but it did not succeed. In 1933, when I went to Shanghai for the first time, I was brought to the work center to work together with the brothers. At that time, we had already encountered this problem of the change of the system that is being spoken of today. We were considering how to eliminate the meeting with one speaking and the rest listening, and change to all the saints going out to preach the gospel. Eventually, after much effort, we could not find a workable way. In 1937 Brother Watchman Nee released a series of messages concerning re-thinking our work. He emphatically said that the Lord's Day message meeting was a waste, and that this meeting was following the customs of the nations; it was not worth maintaining. In 1948, in the book *Church Affairs*, he mentioned this matter again, and the words he used were much stronger than those spoken eleven years earlier. For thirty-six years, from 1949, when I was sent to Taiwan to spread the Lord's work overseas, until 1984, when I returned to

Taiwan, this matter of changing the system has been an unresolved problem in our midst.

Within that period, from the time of Brother Nee's imprisonment in 1952 until his death in prison in 1972, we cannot say that he had any work; also, we had no way to correspond with him. By the Lord's mercy I simply had to coordinate with the brothers and sisters to spread the work of the Lord's recovery overseas. In the areas from Taiwan to Southeast Asia, and from Southeast Asia to Japan, I spent over ten years' effort. After that, most of my time was spent in the western world in developing the work in America, Europe, Africa, and Australia. In the last approximately twenty years, we have established over six hundred churches. Including the development in Asia, there are over nine hundred churches on the whole earth at the present time.

Three years ago, I was alerted by the practical situations. I discovered that, although the Lord's recovery had spread to the six continents, no matter which place it had spread to, that place soon became stagnant. Nearly every place was like this. The situation that bothered me the most was that of the United States. From 1962 to 1984, twenty-two years altogether, I was there carrying out the work personally. I traveled from the south to the north, from the east coast to the west coast, to the extent that today there is a church in the Lord's recovery in nearly all the big cities. There are altogether about one hundred churches; the number is not too small. However, regarding the increase in number, we have nothing to boast about. In the first ten years, there was still a twenty to thirty percent increase rate, but in the last ten years, the average increase rate was only three percent. One of the areas that burdened me most heavily was Orange County, California, where I live. From the time we moved there in 1974 until 1984, ten years altogether, the number has not increased.

However, you need to understand that in the last ten years, I spent half a year's time each year (three months in the first half of the year, and three months in the second half) in writing, composing the footnotes of the New Testament, and also revising the translated text of the English version of the Bible. Besides these, there were the semi-annual trainings held to expound the New Testament book by book, resulting in the Life-study Messages of the Bible. These occupied at least two-thirds of my time. The time that was left was limited; hence, I had no way to take care of the needs in the various local churches. In 1984, after I had completed the footnotes of all the books of the New Testament, I decided to come back to Taipei. As soon as I came back, I mentioned this important issue of changing the system. At that time, I said that we started this change of the system on a trial basis, and we did not need others' criticism or adjustment. We ourselves knew how to adjust as we went on. While I was learning the way of the recovery from Brother Watchman Nee, I acquired the skill of making adjustments. Because this new way has never been taken by anyone, we may be considered as pioneers. Hence, everything requires study and improvement.

THE INCLUSIVENESS OF THE NEW WAY

When we began to take this way, we were not quite sure of the way of doing things; however, we have seen quite clearly the principle and the emphasis. I held on to one thing: the principle cannot be changed, and the emphasis cannot be shifted; the truth is forever the truth. My principle and emphasis are Christ, the Spirit, life, and the church. Although my voice for changing the system and walking the new way was very high and strong, I walked very firmly in a stable way. I walked slowly, step by step, according to my evaluation of the church's situation and the pace of the brothers. I was like a cook, busy working in the kitchen every day, preparing to put forth a feast. Therefore, I hope that no one will be anxious. You cannot require that we succeed within three years in this change of the system which has not been successfully accomplished within the last fifty years. You need to wait patiently and broaden your view. You also need to listen accurately and should not assume that your understanding is the same as what I spoke. I found that the people outside the training were not clear, or misunderstood, or had too many opinions concerning the change of the system. Even with those who were in the training, there were areas where they did not listen accurately, or understand adequately. They may have listened correctly and understood rightly, but when they went out to speak, they did not speak accurately. Therefore, now I feel compelled to present the inclusiveness of the new way in its entirety so that you can have a complete view.

In the Objective Aspect of the Truth— Christ, the Spirit, Life, and the Church

We should realize that the Lord's recovery is to recover Christ, the Spirit, life, and the church. Christ is the embodiment and expression of the Triune God; He is the all-inclusive God-man. Concerning this point, *Hymns* #501 has given a simple, clear, and appropriate description. The Spirit is the ultimate expression of the Triune God. The theology in Christianity has separated God into three Persons: the Father being one Person, the Son being one Person, and the Spirit being another Person. But we see from the Bible that Christ is the embodiment of God and is not separate from the Father. He Himself says, "I and the Father are one" (John 10:30). Then, again, He says, "You, Father, are in Me and I in You" (John 17:21). The Bible also says that the Holy Spirit is the reality of the Son (John 14:17-20; 1 John 5:6). Hence, the Father, the Son, and the Spirit are one. This Triune God has passed through incarnation, human living, crucifixion, and resurrection from the dead, and He has become the life-giving Spirit (1 Cor. 15:45). Therefore, now the Lord is the Spirit (2 Cor. 3:17). At the end of the Bible it says, "The Spirit and the bride say, Come!" (Rev. 22:17). The Spirit here is the ultimate expression of the processed Triune God. Moreover, life is simply Christ, and life is also the Spirit. In John 14, Christ says, "I am the life." This Christ who is life, having passed through the processes to become the life-giving Spirit, entered into us to be the life that we enjoy.

Romans 8:2 speaks of "the Spirit of life." This term joins life together with the Spirit, which indicates that everything related to life is contained within the Spirit. Life belongs to the Spirit; and the Spirit is of life. These two are one in reality. Hence, Christ is the Spirit, and the Spirit is life. The Spirit entering into us is the Triune God being our eternal and incorruptible life. When this life is gained by us, the result is the producing of the church, and the ultimate consummation of the church is the New Jerusalem. The sixty-six books of the entire Bible begin with God, the Triune God, and consummate in the New Jerusalem. And the New Jerusalem is the ultimate manifestation of the mingling of the processed Triune God with the redeemed and transformed tripartite man.

This is our vision, and it is the objective truth in the Lord's recovery. I have released over two thousand messages concerning Christ, the Spirit, life, and the church. These messages have also been published as books. I hope that the younger generation and the newcomers to the Lord's recovery would spend time to study these messages.

In the Subjective Aspect of Practice

Preaching the Gospel

We have already covered the new way in the objective aspect of the truth. Concerning the subjective aspect of practice, the first item is preaching the gospel. Every saved one is willing to preach the gospel. Among us we paid attention to this matter from the very beginning. However, in the recent ten years, from 1975 to 1984, we cannot deny that the effect of our gospel preaching was not that great. We in the Lord's recovery must bear this responsibility.

The Increase in the Lord's Recovery
Being at a Standstill for the Last Ten Years

In 1949, the Lord's recovery went overseas. Under my leadership, the recovery first reached Taiwan, then Southeast Asia, then Japan, and finally the Western World. I personally experienced and witnessed the spread of the Lord's recovery. By 1975, within twenty-six years, the number had increased considerably. Just take Taiwan as an example: the number increased from four or five hundred to over forty thousand. It was exactly a one hundredfold increase. But in the ten-year period from 1975 to 1984, there was nearly no increase; the number was at a standstill. I started working in the United States in 1962. After thirteen years, the number had increased from one or two hundred to over ten thousand. Although the increase cannot be considered rapid, it was still somewhat comforting. However, in the last ten years, the number has hardly increased. It was first the situation of Taiwan, then that of the United States, which burdened me very much. Concerning Canada, the brothers there have worked for nearly twenty years, but the number now is still not quite one thousand. Regarding Europe, there were originally only a few people. After 1971, some brothers went there, and the door of the Lord's recovery was opened. In 1984, of the number in all of Europe, Germany had the greatest number, followed by Switzerland and England. Then there were other countries including France, Italy, and Denmark. The total number did not exceed eight hundred. Concerning Australia and New Zealand, I went there in 1971. By 1984, the total number of the two places was not more than 300. Speaking of Africa, as early as 1971, the brothers there had very good fellowship with us, and they began to have a testimony of the Lord in Ghana. Up until now, they have already spread to five or six other countries in Africa. The total number exceeds one thousand, but it is still not very satisfactory. In South America, only Brazil had some increase. Up until 1984, the number was not more than two thousand people. In Central and South America, a total of more than twenty countries, the number still did not exceed ten thousand.

I place this matter before you; if you had a genuine concern and foresight for the interest of the Lord's recovery, how would you feel? When I saw this situation in 1984, I was already eighty years old. I believe that I had received the Lord's special grace and mercy, that I had already reached the age of a strong person as spoken of in the Bible (Psa. 90:10). You may say that what I have now is an extra life given to me by the Lord. When I was contemplating the Lord's recovery on the earth, besides not knowing how to give account when I meet the Lord, I even felt that I could not give account to my former co-worker Brother Nee when I meet him. He had brought us this way and had rendered me the greatest help and a considerable commission. We had worked for so many years; yet, in spite of the fact that there are churches in the five continents, we are at a standstill as far as increase is concerned. How can this not distress me? It does not make me happy to consider the United States; to think of Taiwan, my heart breaks. I had labored here for over ten years, and had accumulated quite a spiritual heritage for so many who love the Lord; yet after you have worked here for twenty more years, you have come to such a result. When I returned three years ago, I came with an aching heart. And as I considered North America, Europe, New Zealand, and Australia, they were not an encouragement to me. I do not feel there is anything to be proud of at all; rather, I feel the time is late, and my remaining years are few. We co-workers in every locality should all prostrate ourselves before the Lord, confess our uselessness, and also ask the Lord for His mercy.

I am one who is bearing a heavy burden, and one who speaks honestly and means business. I am not elevating myself nor am I proud. I am not deceiving myself. According to my knowledge, just in the Philippines and Singapore, there are some large congregations other than ours. In Seoul, Korea alone, there is a congregation with a membership of a few hundred thousand. Although we have churches all over the different continents and countries, as far as the number is concerned, we have hardly anything worth talking about. Therefore, when I returned in 1984 to change the system, the main message was on the increase and spread of the church. This started the practice of gospel preaching by door-knocking.

Warnings from Church History

Within the past three years, we conducted much research. We know that before the Reformation by Luther, there was only one great unified church, the Catholic Church. By seeing the truth, Luther initiated the Reformation movement. This produced the Protestant churches. Nevertheless, it did not take long for them to fall into a situation of deadness and dryness. Afterwards, in the Catholic Church, a group of lovers and seekers of the Lord including Madame Guyon was raised up. They were the so-called Mystics. Due to the Mystics being too mysterious, Andrew Murray later improved their practice and produced the inner life group. At the end of the last century and the beginning of this century, this group was quite prosperous; many received help from them. Then, after that, there was Mrs. Penn-Lewis who had a particular revelation concerning the death of Christ. Following her, Mr. T. Austin-Sparks, her young co-worker, went further to see the principle of the resurrection life. The revelations seen by these two were historic, but regretfully they died barren. Among the Christians on the earth today, there are not many who know about them. Along the line of the Protestant churches, some who saw the matter of presbytery set up the Presbyterian church; some who saw the matter of baptism by immersion set up the Baptist church. Similarly, many groups were raised up. However, at the end, not one of them had a way to go on. Then the Brethren were raised up; they emphasized very much the expounding of the Bible, and were very prosperous in the last century. However, not much later, they were divided due to different opinions. From then on, they continued to divide, and finally, they reached a "dead end." Afterwards, there was the Pentecostal movement. Due to their excessive emphasis on the Pentecostal things, eventually they were also declining. God's economy is all-inclusive; it is not merely a matter of the inner life, nor of a Pentecostal movement. Whoever emphasizes only one aspect will find that their road reaches a "dead end."

Concerning the situation among us, since the time we

left mainland China, I have been presenting to all of you Christ, the Spirit, life, and the church. The brothers have all received what I have presented and have obtained much help. Because of these truths, when we went to different places, we were able to raise up local churches. Also, of the churches raised up in the four continents outside of Asia, eighty to ninety percent were raised up due to the help obtained from the publications of the Living Stream Ministry. They have not only received the points of the truth, but have also stood firm. However, they neglected the matter of preaching the gospel. In the first few years of our work in Taiwan, every training emphasized five matters: the Holy Spirit, the gospel, the church, the service, and the truth. Afterwards, although we still had the preaching of the gospel, it was in the old way of inviting people to the meeting hall to listen to the gospel. After a few decades, what we were doing eventually became a routine without any effect. Due to this situation, we were compelled to find another way.

The Way of Preaching the Gospel as Revealed in the Bible

When we came back to the Bible, we found in it the way to visit people by going to their homes. We then began to go out to knock on doors to preach the gospel and baptize people. When we went to knock on doors, as soon as we preached the gospel, within fifteen minutes, people were baptized, having been saved and regenerated. When they first heard this, most people would have questioned it. Therefore, I did a thorough study of this matter at the very beginning. First, Matthew chapter thirteen shows us that when the Lord went out to sow, there were four kinds of situations with different results. With the first kind, the seeds fell along the wayside and were devoured by the birds. This clearly refers to people who have heard the gospel but who are not yet saved or regenerated. With the second kind, the seeds fell on the rocky places where they did not have much earth; after having sprouted, they withered away. This speaks of a person who was regenerated due to the word of the gospel, but not adequately saved in life day by day. With the third kind, the seeds fell on the thorns. This speaks of a person who has been regenerated and saved, and has some growth in life but has not yet grown up. With the fourth kind, the seeds fell on the good earth and gave fruit. This kind of person is not only saved, but also has the growth and maturity in life, and is bearing fruit. Here the Lord did not tell us that the longer you hear the gospel, the more secure and thorough your salvation will be. It is very difficult to say that the salvation of those who heard the gospel and were baptized quickly is not secure.

Acts 16 talks about two cases of salvation. The first case was concerning a woman who was selling purple-dyed goods. She listened and gave heed to the things spoken by Paul. Later, she and her household were saved (vv. 14-15). It does not say how long she listened; but one thing is certain—after hearing the gospel she was baptized that same day. The second case was concerning the salvation of the jailor and his household (vv. 19-34). When Paul and Silas spoke the Lord's word to the jailor and his whole household, they were immediately baptized that night. In principle, this is the same as when you go out to visit people by knocking on their doors, preach to them *The Mystery of Human Life*, and then baptize them into the Triune God.

For two thousand years, the various denominations and groups have had different views concerning how a person can become a Christian. However, no one has the assurance to say how long a person has to listen to the gospel before he can be saved. It is very difficult to decide to what extent a person should believe in Jesus before he can be acknowledged as a brother. I am here leading the church, helping the brothers to go out to knock on doors to preach the gospel. I said that as long as a person heard the gospel, believed, repented, confessed his sins, admitted that he was a sinner, called upon the name of the Lord Jesus, and was baptized into Christ, then according to the Bible, he is a saved person (Mark 16:16). This matter is not in your hand or in mine; it is in the Lord's hand. When the Ethiopian eunuch was reading Isaiah in his chariot, Philip went up to him, and from that portion of the Word, he preached to him Jesus as the gospel. Afterwards, the eunuch himself said, "Look, water! What prevents me from being baptized?" (Acts 8:26-39). This proves that as long as a person hears the gospel and believes, he can be baptized. On the day of Pentecost, there were three thousand people who received the apostles' word, and they were baptized immediately.

No one has ever been able to say definitely to what extent a person needs to reach in order to be saved. In the same way, no one dares to decide who is a real believer and who is a false believer. This can be likened to people trying to distinguish wheat from tares, which is very difficult unless you wait until the time of harvest. Therefore, God gave the gospel to us, and we simply go to preach it. The Bible says, "Whoever calls upon the name of the Lord shall be saved" (Rom. 10:13). It does not say how long we have to call, or to what degree we have to call. Hence, it is sufficient for us to lead people to call. The Bible says also, "Believe on the Lord Jesus, and you shall be saved, you and your household" (Acts 16:31). Therefore, we simply need to preach and lead whole families to believe in the Lord. Moreover, we need to baptize people according to what the Bible says, "He who believes and is baptized shall be saved" (Mark 16:16). However, even though we preach the gospel and lead people to call and be baptized within fifteen minutes, we should not do it in a hurry or with compulsion. When we lead people to believe in the Lord, we should do it with assurance and with wisdom.

Establishing Home Meetings

Visiting people's homes by door knocking for preaching the gospel is our first step. Immediately following that is the establishing of home meetings. Your baptizing a person equals giving him birth. You have the responsibility to feed him and take care of him; otherwise, it will be very easy for him to have an early death. Therefore, you need to set up a home meeting immediately in the new believer's home. In order to establish home meetings, you need to start first with your own home to have home meetings with your own wife or husband and children to live a normal church life. In this way, you can lead the newly saved ones to have home meetings and to live a normal church life.

Speaking to One Another
and Listening to One Another

Following that, you need to practice speaking to one another and listening to one another in the meetings. Regardless of whether they are large meetings or small meetings, we need to stay away from the habit of one speaking and the rest listening. We must overthrow this tradition of Christianity and change to speaking to one another and listening to one another. In order to achieve this, we need to endeavor together and have a spiritual and victorious living daily. We need to live in spirit every day and fellowship with the Lord moment by moment, in order to be filled with the Spirit inwardly and outwardly. By this we can go to the new ones' homes to lead them to enjoy the Lord together. Therefore, to live a spiritual and victorious life is very necessary. Anyone who does not live a spiritual and victorious life is through with his church life and service.

Building Up the Local Churches
for the Building Up of the Body of Christ

Up to this point, you can realize that the new way is not merely knocking on doors for preaching the gospel, nor does it stop at building up home meetings. The new way further requires us to be living persons who can speak and also listen. Hence, we all need to have a spiritual and victorious living, live in spirit moment by moment, walk according to the Spirit, and be burning in spirit. Eventually, all these are not for ourselves, but for the establishing of the local churches for the building up of the Body of Christ, which is the universal church. This is the practice of the new way in the subjective aspect. This begins with the dispensing of the Triune God into people that they may receive Him, call upon His name, and be baptized into His name. It continues with the feeding and caring for people and the establishing of home meetings in their homes to eventually build up the local churches.

May we all see that the new way is the way of the Lord's recovery. The new way is inclusive. It starts with knocking on doors for preaching the gospel to dispense the Triune God into people; then it continues with establishing home meetings in the believers' homes, with speaking to one another and listening to one another, for the building up of the local churches. When we are building the local churches in this way, we are building up the Body of Christ, the universal church. I hope that you all can listen to this word completely, thoroughly, and comprehensively. When you return to your respective localities to speak, you must also speak completely, thoroughly, and comprehensively. May the Lord have mercy on us!

A message given by Brother Witness Lee in Taipei on November 2, 1987.

CHAPTER SIXTEEN

THE INCLUSIVENESS OF THE NEW WAY

(2)

Scripture Reading: Matt. 20:9-14; Luke 14:23

THE KEY TO THE MEETINGS IN THE NEW WAY

As a continuation of the preceding message, I would like to add a few final words. The most important item in the new way is the matter of meetings. The problem with the meetings is not whether they are big or small, but whether they have one person speaking with the rest listening or everyone speaking and listening to one another. This is the key to the meetings and also the focus of the problem.

We know that most of the gatherings in society are carried out with one person speaking and the rest listening. This is the worldly way. The basic principle in any of the meetings called by the worldly people is one person speaking and the rest listening. At best, there are only two or three speakers with the rest listening, but the principle is still the same. As early as 1948 Brother Watchman Nee spoke concerning this matter. In the book *Church Affairs*, he said that to maintain the Lord's Day morning meeting is to follow the customs of the nations. He quoted this from 2 Kings 17:8, which says, "Walked in the customs of the nations" (RSV). We can see from the context of this verse that this was referring to the gatherings of God's people to worship God by following the customs of the nations. According to the types and the revelation in the Bible, the proper gatherings of God's people, especially the three annual feasts, were meetings where everyone would bring one-tenth of their rich produce, the choice and the topmost part, to offer to God. Thus all could enjoy these portions together with God and before God. This enjoyment was altogether mutual. This matter has been very clearly presented in the messages we have released and even in our hymnals.

THE PRINCIPLE OF CHRISTIAN MEETINGS

According to the revelation in the New Testament, the meetings of God's children are also in the principle of mutuality. Even when the whole church is gathered together, it should be, and must be, in this manner, that is, "each one has" (1 Cor. 14:26). You speak, he speaks, I speak, and everyone speaks. Moreover, when one speaks, everyone listens. Everyone is speaking to one another and listening to one another. This is the governing principle of the meetings in God's New Testament economy. Whether a Christian meeting is according to the desire of God's heart or not does not depend upon the condition of the meeting, but upon the principle on which the meeting is based. In that meeting is there the practice of one person speaking with the rest listening, or is there the practice of speaking to one another and listening to one another?

The desire of God's heart is that all His people would speak God's word. Numbers 11 shows us that God descended in the cloud and spoke to Moses. He also took of the Spirit that had fallen upon Moses and gave it to the seventy elders of the people so that they could also speak as prophets. Among them were two persons who prophesied in the camp. When Joshua found out about it, he wanted Moses to forbid them. But Moses said, "Would God that all the Lord's people were prophets" (v. 29). In the same principle, Paul in 1 Corinthians 14 also said, "You can all prophesy one by one" (v. 31). This is the principle of Christian meetings: everyone can speak for God. Only the meetings in this principle are according to God's desire, are of the New Testament, and are in God's economy. Moreover, only this kind of meeting is not secular and is separated from the world.

THE MAJOR OUTLINE FOR SPEAKING IN THE MEETINGS

It is not an easy thing to have everyone speaking in the

meeting. It is easy to have a meeting with one person speaking and the rest listening as long as you can find a speaker and have the seats ready. However, it is difficult to have every attendant speak because in the Christian meetings one should not speak ordinary words, but the words of God.

To speak the word of God we have to first speak of the Triune God. Second, we have to speak of Christ who is the Triune God having become flesh. Third, we have to speak of the Spirit who is the ultimate manifestation of the Triune God. Fourth, we have to speak about the spiritual life. And fifth, we also have to speak about the church. Concerning the church, there are two aspects: the universal church and the local church. The universal church is the Body of Christ, while the local church is the local expression of this unique Body in the universe. These items are the major outline for the speaking for God in the meetings.

Besides these, we also have to speak that God is holy, righteous, and glorious, and that because of this, He has the requirements of holiness, righteousness, and glory. At the same time, we also have to speak about man. Man is of three parts: spirit, soul, and body. When God created man, He gave man a good nature. But man fell, and the evil nature of Satan entered into man to become the sinful nature in man. Because of this, man also has sinful deeds outwardly. I just describe these to show you what you should speak in the meetings. In addition, the hymns are also a very good means for speaking because they are God's words composed into poetry and songs. The words are simple but rich in meaning. They inspire feeling easily and can also be used for speaking to one another.

SPEAKING THE WORD OF GOD REQUIRING TRAINING

Today's problem is that from the beginning our brothers and sisters did not have this practice, nor have they endeavored in this area. Therefore, the people whom we have nurtured for the last few decades know how to listen but not how to speak. They have no problem speaking the worldly things when they are at home. However, as soon as they come to the meetings, they become speechless knowing just to listen and not to speak. Some would listen and at the same time criticize in their hearts. But, when they are asked to speak, they cannot say anything. Although many brothers and sisters know some truths, they are unable to speak them. They can only perform some practical services. Eventually, there are not many in the church who have had the training to speak for God. Concerning this, we have failed miserably. For this reason, to ask the brothers and sisters to build up home meetings now would be as difficult as climbing a high mountain. In the past, it was easy to have the meetings with one person speaking and the rest listening. Such meetings could be held any time. Presently, for every attendant to speak the word of God in the meetings is not easy; yet, only this kind of meeting is rich and glorious. However this kind of situation cannot be brought in overnight. For over thirty years, we have been meeting, but we have not established the habit of everyone speaking the Lord's word. Having everyone speak now would be like requiring us to speak English instantly when we have been speaking Chinese for the past few decades. It is extremely difficult. For this very reason, we have been here trying to change the system for three years and have not yet succeeded.

BEING AN OVERCOMER AND TAKING THE WAY OF THE LORD'S RECOVERY

We should not merely speak in the meetings, but we should also speak with the Spirit. When we speak, we bring forth the Spirit. To have something to say, all one needs to do is to learn; but to have the Spirit in one's speaking, one needs to live in the Spirit every moment. Therefore, this kind of meeting with speaking to one another and listening to one another requires every one of us to be an overcomer. There is no need of this for the worship services in Christianity. For us to speak for God in the meetings, with the word and the Spirit, we must overcome and we must be living. We need to store up the Lord's word daily to let the Lord's word be added to our being in our daily living, and we need to live in the spirit moment by moment. In this way, we will be overcomers, full of the word and of the Spirit. Then, when we come to the meetings, spontaneously the word and the Spirit will spring out from within us.

If the church here has not brought the brothers and sisters into this victorious realm, where each one is full of the word and of the Spirit, it will be impossible to ask everyone to speak to one another and listen to one another in the meetings. In the end, we would need to find a preacher to substitute for us: this is a downhill way. It is always difficult to go uphill and easy to go downhill. Today all of Christianity is going downhill and slipping; but we must take the way of recovery and go uphill. We need to read the Lord's word daily, exercise our spirit moment by moment, and live in the spirit. As long as we do this, to have everyone speak in the meetings will not be an impossible task because the Lord's supply and preparation will indeed be sufficient.

In the Lord's recovery, this new way has three important points of practice. First, the gospel preaching must be effective. Then, the meetings must be full of the word and the Spirit, with speaking to one another and listening to one another. Finally, the churches must be built up locally. These three points are lacking in our midst, not to mention that they are non-existent in the denominations of Christianity. Today, all the brothers and sisters in the Lord's recovery need to humble themselves and confess to the Lord that in these three important points of God's New Testament economy, we have been a failure. First, our gospel preaching has not been effective: instead of increasing each year, there has been only stagnation. In October of 1984, I returned to Taipei; the messages I gave in the first conference were on the increase and spread of the churches. Until today, I have not changed my slogan; it remains the same. Regardless of whether our way of gospel preaching by door knocking is good or not, every saint in the Lord's recovery must admit to the fact that our way of gospel preaching in the past was ineffective. Second, to this day, the principle of our meetings is still basically that one person speaks and the rest listen. We still do not meet according to the revelation of the New Testament. Third, as far as the building up of the church is concerned, we have the truth, but not much practical building. Because we have not done well with the second main point, that of the building up of individuals, we cannot yet speak of the building up of the church.

RECEIVING IN HUMILITY AND STUDYING IN ONE ACCORD FOR THE ACCOMPLISHMENT OF THE LORD'S NEW WAY

Finally, I have to point out one more matter. Since I returned to change the system in 1984, I have repeatedly declared that because we have not walked in this new way that much, what we are doing here is on a trial basis. We need a lot of study, with the training center of the full-timers as our laboratory. Whatever we have done is not final. Therefore people should not criticize what our training does, because it is not the final stage, and it is not yet the time for judgment. A wise person will definitely not do such a thing. I can tell you that this experiment is not for me, but for the Lord's recovery on the earth today. This experiment is not for one local church, but for all the churches on the whole earth. It is not merely for this generation, but also for the generations to come. Therefore, let those who are in one accord with us and who are humble walk this way, labor diligently, and study every aspect together with us.

I have more or less discharged my burden at this point. I hope that none of those who have received training here will consider himself perfected. You should know that you are merely a student doing research in a laboratory and that the final results of our research have not yet been obtained. Hence, you should not boast of what you have learned here. When you return to your respective places, you have to be humble and show that what you know is limited. One thing I know for certain—all of Christianity has failed, and even we ourselves are not that victorious.

Our gospel preaching is not prevailing; the meetings are not carried out properly; and the building up of the church has not been adequate. We must bow our heads and admit these three severe shortcomings. We look to the Lord for His mercy that for the sake of His Body He would grant us a way to overcome these failures. Let us be humble and empty ourselves to receive the Lord's leading.

A message given by Brother Witness Lee in Taipei on November 3, 1987.

CHAPTER SEVENTEEN

LEARNING TO SPEAK THE LORD'S WORD AND TEACHING OTHERS TO SPEAK THE LORD'S WORD

Scripture Reading: 2 Tim. 3:15-17; Col. 3:16; Eph. 5:18; 1 Thes. 5:20

This morning we will consider the focal point of the change of the system, which is the speaking of the Lord's word. The degradation and failure of Christianity and its greatest lack lies in the fact that the believers do not speak the Lord's word. The principle of the New Testament is that every saved person is a member of the Body of Christ and a priest of God. As such, everyone should serve God and speak for God. Therefore, we all have to learn to speak the Lord's word and to teach others to do the same.

ORIGINALLY BORN IN ADAM TO SPEAK FOR ADAM

We were all originally born in Adam to be the descendants of Adam, a part of Adam, and even the members of Adam. It does not matter in which country we were born and what language we speak; we are speaking for Adam, and are even speaking Adam. It does not matter whether one belongs to a high class speaking refined words, or to a low class speaking coarse words; he is speaking Adam. The whole world is a kingdom of Adam, a sphere of Adam. This was our condition not merely before we were saved, but even after we were saved, it could be possible that we still speak for Adam.

AFTER SALVATION THERE STILL BEING THE LACK OF THE REALITY IN CHRIST

After we were saved and regenerated, we were transferred from Adam into Christ and joined to Christ, to become members of Christ. The vision and light are very clear among us, but we are short of a living in Christ. The revelation and the teachings are here, but the reality is lacking. If we do not live in Christ, we may be in Christ in name, but in reality we are still in Adam. The only difference is that before salvation we were free to sin; but now, after salvation, and especially after we are stirred up to love the Lord and are brought into the church life, we begin to refrain from sinful things and to behave more properly. But in our daily walk we are still in Adam.

In Paul's Epistles, the believers are exhorted to refrain from murmurings and reasonings (Phil. 2:14). They are also exhorted not to judge (1 Cor. 4:5). This shows us that there were often many such things among the brothers and sisters at that time. In Greek the word for *reasoning* has the sense of arguing and debating. Today even among the churches in the Lord's recovery, it is still difficult to avoid reasoning, arguing, and debating. In Colossians, Paul even said that there were complaints one against another (Col. 3:13a). If there are complaints among us, this proves that we are not living in Christ. If we live in Christ, we will be closely knitted together, but if we live in Adam, there will be complaints, opinions, and frictions. All these things are in Adam, proving that we are speaking for Adam. We do not have to learn to speak for Adam. All of us are perfect representatives of Adam.

LEARNING THE TRUTH IN ORDER TO SPEAK FOR THE LORD

Since we are saved and are the members of Christ, it is reasonable that we should speak for the Lord; however, most of us are still not speaking. This is because we lack the knowledge of the truth. Therefore, the Bible tells us that God "desires all men to be saved and come to the full knowledge of the truth" (1 Tim. 2:4). As soon as a person is saved, he should learn the truth and should come to the full knowledge of the truth. When we were born, we knew nothing of the truth. Even after we become a Christian, if we do not learn the truth, we will not know the Lord, and consequently we will not be able to speak for the Lord. For this reason, immediately after we are saved, we should learn the truth; then we will be able to speak God's word in Christ.

EXAMPLES IN THE NEW TESTAMENT
CONCERNING SPEAKING

Luke 1 records three examples of speaking for the Lord. The first one is Elizabeth, the mother of John the Baptist; the second is Mary, the mother of the Lord Jesus; and the third is Zachariah, the father of John the Baptist. When Elizabeth was filled with the Holy Spirit, she lifted up her voice with a loud cry and said to Mary, "Blessed are you among women, and blessed is the fruit of your womb! And how can this be, that the mother of my Lord should come to me? For behold, when the sound of your greeting came to my ears, the baby leaped in my womb with exultation. And blessed is she who believed, because there shall be a completion of the things spoken to her from the Lord" (vv. 42-45). Although Elizabeth's word is short, it is very sweet and rich. Her blessing by the Holy Spirit reveals that the Savior in His humanity is the "fruit" and in His deity is the "Lord." She recognized the fruit of Mary's womb as her Lord, and acknowledged the deity of the Child to be born of Mary (Psa. 110:1; Matt. 22:43-45). How different is this kind of speaking from the so-called outpouring of the Holy Spirit and the tongue-speaking in the Pentecostal movement! Most of their tongue-speaking is, "My people, the time is short! Behold, I come quickly. There will be an earthquake in such and such a place, and the whole city will go into the ocean!" They speak this kind of word because these are the words they receive all the time. They are always listening to these words; therefore, when they receive the so-called outpouring of the Holy Spirit, they spontaneously speak these words. None of them can give a concise word of revelation as Elizabeth did.

Next, let us look at Mary's speaking. Mary said, "My soul magnifies the Lord, and my spirit has exulted in God my Savior; because He has looked upon the low estate of

His slave. For behold, from now on all generations will count me blessed; because the Mighty One has done great things for me, and holy is His name; and His mercy is unto generations and generations to those who fear Him. He has done mighty things with His arm; He has scattered those who are proud in the understanding of their heart. He brought down potentates from thrones and exalted the humble. He has filled the hungry with good things, and the rich He sent away empty. He has succored Israel His servant to remember mercy, even as He spoke to our fathers, to Abraham and to his seed forever" (Luke 1:46-55). Mary's word is not too long, yet it is very rich. Almost every sentence is quoted from the Old Testament. She put crucial points from the Old Testament together to produce a psalm of praise. Doubtless, she must have been very familiar with the Old Testament. Not only so, she must have been well exercised in it. With such a person who is full of God's word within and well exercised in these words, God's word will flow out from within him as soon as the Holy Spirit is poured out. If today the Holy Spirit is poured out upon you as He was upon Mary, I am afraid that you will not be able to speak the same words as Mary did because you lack God's word in your daily life.

Lastly, let us take a look at the long psalm of Zachariah. When Zachariah was filled with the Holy Spirit, he prophesied, saying, "Blessed be the Lord, the God of Israel, because He has visited and accomplished redemption for His people, and raised a horn of salvation for us in the house of David His servant, even as He spoke through the mouth of His holy prophets from of old— salvation from our enemies, and out of the hand of all those who hate us; to show mercy to our fathers, and to remember His holy covenant, the oath which He swore to Abraham our father, to grant us that, having been delivered out of the hand of our enemies, we might serve Him without fear, in holiness and righteousness before Him all our days. And you also, young child, shall be called a prophet of the Most High, for you will go before the Lord to prepare His ways, to give knowledge of salvation to His people in forgiveness of their sins, because of the merciful compassions of our God, in which the rising sun from on high shall visit us, to appear to those sitting in darkness and in the shadow of death, to guide our feet into the way of peace" (vv. 68-79). After reading this portion of the Word, we will realize that for anyone to speak such a long psalm he must be very familiar with the Bible!

THE WAY OF CHRISTIANITY CHOKING TO DEATH THE FUNCTION OF THE BELIEVERS

We have already mentioned that Christians are those who speak for the Lord. Whenever Christians are gathered together, their meeting should be for speaking the Lord's word. However, it is not that easy for everyone to speak this way. As a result, a clerical class of pastors and preachers is gradually produced. These people have studied theology specifically and are the professional speakers for the Lord. Once the clerical class is brought forth, the situation of one speaking and the rest listening is produced. This practice of one speaking and the rest listening best fits peoples' situation because no one needs to labor, and it eliminates the trouble of learning the Lord's word. Everyone can then be busy all day long with their secular business; all they need to do is come to a meeting on Sunday. In the meeting they do not need to open their mouths. Professionals like the pastors and preachers who have been trained in theology will come to speak. These ones speak with skill, persuasion, and eloquence. They are too good. This kind of meeting with one speaking and the rest listening may help people superficially, but actually it chokes to death the function of all the members.

When I was in my hometown at the age of twenty-two or twenty-three, I loved the Lord and sought after Him very much. One day I attended a Bible study meeting. I sat on the last row, thinking that no one would notice me. To my surprise, the one that went to the podium that day was the founder of that Bible study group. He knew me very well. After reading the Scriptures he said, "Today we would like to invite Mr. Witness Lee to pray." I was so shaken that I forgot where I was. I did not know how to start the prayer. At that time I already loved the Lord very much. I studied the Word a lot, read many reference books, and took a lot of notes. But for me to pray before two to three hundred people was something that I had never done before. I believe that many of you have had the same experience as I did. This is the situation in Christianity. A person may be very seeking yet still be unable to pray in the meeting.

On another occasion I was meeting with the Independent Church of Christ in China. The pastor there had a high regard for me and invited me to preach at a large worship service on a Lord's Day morning. For that I spent a week or two practicing at the seaside, where nobody could see me, speaking to the ocean over and over again. Then I became somewhat confident of my speaking. But when I stepped onto the platform that Lord's Day morning, my knees were shaking. I forgot nearly everything except the Lord Jesus Christ and His cross. I managed to piece together my message, speaking for about forty minutes, and hurriedly left the stage. Although I loved reading the Bible, took notes for all of my readings, and was very thorough in my studies, yet I felt very uneasy when asked to pray or speak for the Lord. In principle this is the general situation of Christianity, and is even to some extent the situation among us. Many brothers and sisters have loved the Lord for years. They study the Bible, listen to messages, take notes, and are full of riches within. However, they feel uncomfortable when asked to pray or to speak some words for the Lord in the meeting, because they have never been trained in this way.

LEARNING AND PRACTICING TO SPEAK
THE LORD'S WORD

In order to change this situation of one speaking and the rest listening to that of speaking to one another and listening to one another, everyone has to learn to speak the Lord's word. It is easy to talk about this but not easy to practice. To take the old way of Christianity is easy, but to take the God-ordained way in the New Testament is not easy. It requires learning. Everyone has to learn to speak the Lord's word. We all know that speaking is an easy matter; but it requires you to learn when you are young until it becomes habitual through practice. When a mother says to her child, "This is bitter," the child follows by saying, "This is bitter." When the mother says, "This is sweet," the child follows by saying, "This is sweet." By practicing in this way, the child will gradually be able to speak. After a person is saved and is brought into our midst, if from the first day we would teach him to practice speaking the Lord's word in the same way that a mother teaches her child to speak, that one will soon be able to speak. In the past, I could not understand why the brothers and sisters were not willing to speak. Later, I realized that the problem was not that the brothers and sisters were not willing to speak; rather, it was that we have not led them to speak.

I hope that you all would see that the most difficult step in the changing of the system is to have everyone speak in the meeting. If this kind of meeting of speaking to one another and listening to one another is not realized, we do not have the scriptural way to meet. Then we would have to take the old way, still depending on one speaking and the rest listening. But since the Lord has spoken this word in the Bible, surely He will fulfill it. He will change the system from one speaking to everyone speaking. Of course, this requires a lot of labor. To train one Chinese person to speak English is not too difficult, but to train every Chinese person, both young and old, to speak English is very difficult! This is why today we cannot be hasty in changing the system, taking the new way, and getting everyone to speak the Lord's word. I believe that if we would practice this constantly, by the time the next generation rises up, there will be a situation in which it would be difficult to ask them not to speak the Lord's word. Today we are in the transitional stage. If this stage is handled properly, the whole atmosphere will gradually be changed.

During this period, the most important thing is for every one of us to learn and to practice speaking the Lord's word, and to help others to practice speaking the Lord's word. First, this requires that we base our speaking on the Bible. If we want to base our speaking on the Bible, we must be thoroughly familiar with the Bible. In particular, we must familiarize ourselves with the New Testament; otherwise, it will be difficult for us to speak the Lord's word properly. When those in the Pentecostal movement speak in tongues and interpret their tongues, their interpretations never go beyond the few books such as Psalms, Isaiah, and Jeremiah. This is because they, like the Jews, are familiar only with the Old Testament. They have no concept concerning the central vision of the New Testament revealed in such books as Ephesians and Colossians. Therefore, no matter how they experience the outpouring of the Holy Spirit, and no matter how they speak in tongues, they are not able to utter the revelations in Ephesians. This shows us that to learn to speak the Lord's word, we must carefully study the New Testament, especially the book of Ephesians.

Second, we have to learn to speak by means of the hymns. The words of the hymns are also based on the Bible. They are words of the Bible put into poetry and songs. For this reason, we also have to familiarize ourselves with the hymns among us and to bring others into the riches of the hymns.

Third, we have to learn to speak by means of the spiritual publications. Today in the Lord's recovery, there are many spiritual publications that can render us help in the knowledge and experience of the Lord. We also have to spend time to get into these publications so that we will have the rich words.

TEACHING AND LEADING OTHERS
TO SPEAK THE LORD'S WORD

We learn to speak the Lord's word in this way. When we go to the new believers, we also teach them in the same way little by little, just as a mother teaches her child to speak. When a child learns to speak, it may be quite slow at the beginning. He can only utter something word by word; but after two or three years his speaking will consist of sentences and paragraphs.

Hence, after we baptize someone, we should go back to him and help him to know that he is saved. At the same time we have to lead him to know this Savior Jesus Christ. He is God; He is also the Spirit, the ultimate expression of God. In His flesh when He was upon the cross, He was our Redeemer; but today within us He is the Spirit of life. Then we have to open up the book of Romans and tell him, "This Spirit is like the word, so near to you, even in your mouth and in your heart. It is very simple to receive Him. All we need to do is open up our mouth to call on His name with our spirit, saying, 'O Lord Jesus!' His Spirit will then touch our spirit." After we guide him once in this way, he will know how to call on the name of the Lord.

Then we should teach him to pray, "O Lord Jesus, You are my Savior and my life." This is the beginning of his speaking of the Lord. Next we should teach him to read the Bible and acquaint him with terms such as the Triune God, Christ, the Spirit, the church, sanctification, and justification. We should not expect him to learn everything all at once; rather, we have to teach him slowly, little by little.

FOUR GROUPS OF PEOPLE SPEAKING IN THE MEETINGS CAUSING THE CHURCH TO PROGRESS RAPIDLY

Concerning speaking to one another and listening to one another, I think that as long as one quarter of those meeting in the church are willing to practice this, we will have the proper result. Take the church in Taipei as an example. I fully believe that there are one thousand brothers and sisters who will take the lead to practice this way to speak in the meetings. The rest of the brothers and sisters will learn from them. After a period of time, there will surely be great improvements. Among this one thousand people, there are the elders, the co-workers, the full-timers, and the young students, especially the college students. These four groups of people should take the lead to speak in the meetings. Especially the elders, as the head sheep, should take the lead among the flock to practice speaking the Lord's word in the meetings. I believe that if these four groups of people are stirred up in their spirit and would come to the meetings to speak, the church will progress rapidly in the new way.

A message given by Brother Witness Lee in Taipei on November 5, 1987.

CHAPTER EIGHTEEN

EXERCISING TO SPEAK THE LORD'S WORD AT ALL TIMES

Scripture Reading: Eph. 5:18-19; Col. 3:16

The church in Taipei has made the decision to practice the new system in the one hundred "gospel tents" formed during the gospel festival. The word "tent" was a term used temporarily. For the long run, it would be more suitable to use the term "district." The one hundred tents will then be the one hundred districts. In the future, in Taipei we will have the home meetings which have the fewest number of attendants, and we will have the group meetings as a larger kind of meeting. When we combine a few group meetings, we will have the district meeting. Then a few district meetings will be combined to form the hall meeting. When all the hall meetings are combined, we will have the meeting of the whole church.

NO EXAMPLE SEEN IN CHURCH HISTORY OF MEETINGS IN MUTUALITY

When we begin to practice meeting according to the new system, we will be faced with one hurdle: to overthrow the tradition of one speaking and the rest listening, and to change the situation to everyone speaking and everyone listening, to speaking and listening in mutuality. To speak about this is easy, but to practice it is not easy. We have studied almost all of the history of Christianity, the writings of renowned persons, and biographies of spiritual giants. Therefore, we are fairly familiar with what Christianity has passed through during the past twenty centuries, with what they have, and with what the situation among them has been. I have been asking myself during the past few days, "Since the time of the apostles, has there ever been anyone who practiced this kind of meeting of mutuality?" According to my knowledge, there has been none! In other words, it seems that the meeting as revealed in 1 Corinthians 14:26, in which everyone has equal opportunity to speak, has never been put into practice since the apostles' time. For this reason, we cannot find a model of the church meeting.

Since 1934, Brother Watchman Nee had been emphasizing that meetings with one speaking and the rest listening are not scriptural. He said that this was to follow the custom of the nations, that it was unnecessary, and that it should not be maintained. For this reason, he sought earnestly to find the biblical way to practice 1 Corinthians 14:26. He felt that if this kind of meeting with one speaking and the rest listening were removed immediately, there would be nothing to replace it. Hence, he established a brothers' meeting and a sisters' meeting. During these meetings there was no chairman or leader. Everyone could call a hymn, pray, or speak. When this was put into practice, everyone just gave testimonies. Since there had been no such testimony meetings for a long time prior to this, everyone felt that they were fresh and attractive at the beginning. But after a few months, all the testimonies ran out; there was nothing more to speak about. In the end, these meetings just stopped by themselves. In 1949, we also had brothers' meetings and sisters' meetings in Taiwan. The result was again unsatisfactory.

In 1965 I went to visit Brazil. While I was there I visited one free group. The leader of the group had a Pentecostal background. He had the baptism of the Holy Spirit and he spoke in tongues, but he did not bring these things into the big meetings. Even in their small meetings, they did not practice these things very much. They began in 1915. When I visited in 1965, they had already been in Brazil for half a century. Their number was about three hundred thousand. In São Paulo alone they had thirty thousand. In their meetings they did not have any preaching, nor did they use any publications; rather, they had only the Bible. There was absolutely no chairman, pastor, or preacher among them. They did not have any full-timers; everyone held his own job. They did not have a set program for meeting; they only set the day and the time of meeting. Mostly they met on the Lord's Day at nine in the morning. Not long before the time of the meeting, the people would begin to come in. Some would call a hymn. Everyone would then sing together, with the accompaniment of a lot of instruments. They sang for at least half an hour. There was no set line along which they picked the hymns; they simply continued one hymn after another. In an auditorium of seven thousand, they placed only two microphones in the aisles. After the singing they began to come up to testify, the males on one side and the females on the other. They all waited before the microphone for their turn to testify. Sometimes they would testify from nine in the morning until two in the afternoon. After the testimonies, the responsible brother would ask if anyone in the congregation wanted to be baptized. Those that wanted to be baptized had already been saved during their small meetings. Whether the number was large or small, they had baptisms every Lord's Day. Then the leading brother would read a few verses and follow that up with a few words of explanation. After a brief prayer, the meeting was dismissed. This was how they met in big meetings year-round. During the week, they had small group meetings in the vicinity where they lived. There was no preaching in these meetings either; they were all testimony times. These small meetings were mainly for bringing people to be saved, to love the Lord, and to seek after Him. Their speaking also covered subjects that had to do with the details of daily living, such as the way to dress, the way to raise up children, etc. This is one group which I have seen that propagated and increased itself without any preaching meeting.

During the 1960s, there were great improvements in the Pentecostal movement in America. Although they still practiced tongue-speaking, it was not that strongly emphasized; nor were healing and casting out of demons deemed that necessary any longer. In many of their meetings, they had no chairmen or preachers; instead they gave testimonies one after another. In the beginning, this movement was also quite prevailing. Even the Catholics were affected by them. In the 1970s, I personally attended one of their meetings in San Francisco in order to study their situation. The testimonies in their meetings were quite fresh; the spirit of some were indeed revived. But today they also have gradually declined.

According to my observation during these past years, I have not seen many meetings which are according to 1 Corinthians 14:26. Hence, in conclusion I have to say that I have not seen this kind of meeting either in church history or in the spiritual publications or in my own experience. But the Apostle Paul did speak this word in the Bible. There is not only 1 Corinthians 14:26, but there is Hebrews 10:25 as well. The latter also speaks about mutual exhortation in the meetings. I have been a Christian for over sixty years, but I have seen only meetings with the preachers exhorting the congregation. I have not yet seen meetings with the congregation exhorting one another. Therefore up until now, I have seen only the revelation in the Bible; I have not seen any practical example.

MEETINGS OF ONE SPEAKING AND
THE REST LISTENING
NOT PERFECTING THE SAINTS

According to our experience, although the meetings with one speaking and the rest listening can meet certain people's needs and maintain a certain kind of situation, in reality, they do not edify the saints, much less do they perfect the saints as described in Ephesians 4:12. Among us in the past decades, this kind of meeting with one speaking and the rest listening has killed much of the organic function of the brothers and sisters. Consequently, today it is so difficult for them to speak in the meetings. Everyone speaks a lot before the meeting. But once they come into the meeting, they have nothing to speak. Then after the meeting they start speaking again. I have been observing you, the full-timers. Although you do speak in the meetings, your speakings consist only of testimonies or some humorous words. Forgive me for pointing this out, but you have often spoken humorous words to make everyone laugh in the meetings. This is useless. According to Paul's word there are "revelations" and "teachings" and "exhortations." It is interesting that Paul did not mention "testimonies." The problem today is that what the Bible has, the Christians do not have, while what the Bible does not have, the Christians usually have, or would like to have.

THE NEED TO BUILD UP
THE HABIT OF SPEAKING THE LORD'S WORD

This is the reason I told you three years ago that this matter of speaking to one another and listening to one another is a big hurdle. It is a brass door with an iron lock that is very difficult to get through. We have already conducted two terms of training for experimenting and studying the new way. At this point, nothing is in the final form yet; we still need to continue to study. Our training is now in its third term, and the Church in Taipei has been preparing itself for over two years. During this period, although some places have used the *Truth Lessons* as material for mutual speaking in the meetings, I do not yet feel that those meetings are according to 1 Corinthians 14.

Simply speaking, the meeting according to 1 Corinthians 14 is one in which we all speak the Lord's word. We all read the Bible in our daily life. But when we speak, we seldom speak the Scriptures that we have read, and seldom do we speak the Lord's word; we have not yet built up this habit. Luke 1 shows us that when Mary the mother of Jesus went to see Elizabeth, the mother of John, as soon as they met, they opened their mouths to speak the Lord's word; their whole conversation was the Lord's words. Mary did not quote the Scriptures in a dead way; rather, she put together the words of praise in the Old Testament in a living way to comprise a praise to God. This is not something that we can do easily; we have not been guided and taught in this way from the beginning. I have often said that after a child is born, as long as the mother keeps speaking to the child and teaching him, sooner or later, whether the child understands or not, he will be able to speak. But most of us Christians do not have this kind of environment, neither have we seen this kind of situation. All we have seen is someone reading the Scriptures in the meeting and preaching in the meetings. We do not see people speaking the Lord's word in their daily life or in the meetings.

PRACTICING TO SPEAK THE LORD'S WORD WITH THE BIBLE AND BY THE HYMNS

At least ten years ago, I saw that the Bible wants us Christians to speak the Lord's word. Concerning this matter, there are the clear words from the two sister passages in Colossians 3:16 and Ephesians 5:18-19. Ephesians says, "Be filled in spirit, speaking to one another in psalms and hymns and spiritual songs." Colossians says, "Let the word of Christ dwell in you richly, in all wisdom teaching and admonishing one another in psalms, hymns, and spiritual songs." This shows us that Paul taught us to speak the Lord's word. There are two kinds of words of the Lord. One is the words of the Bible; the other is the words of the hymns.

In our experience we do not have the habit of speaking these two kinds of words; therefore, we do not know how to speak. Neither can we find this pattern of practice among Christians during the past nineteen hundred years. For this reason, it is not at all easy for us to speak the words of the Bible and of the hymns in a mutual way in the meetings. This is my heavy burden. Our training here must have a breakthrough in this point. Whenever you go to a meeting, whether large or small, you have to practice speaking mutually to one another with the Bible and by the hymns.

FOUR GROUPS OF PEOPLE PRACTICING THREE THINGS

At present, those brothers and sisters that meet regularly in the church in Taipei still need help. Concerning the practice of the new way, we cannot depend on them yet. Those we can depend on are first, the elders; second, the co-workers; third, the full-timers; and fourth, the college students. These four groups are the main force for the practice of the new way. This morning, you are all among these four groups of people. You have to bear the responsibility of every meeting. The success of the meetings and of the new way in the coming days depends entirely on you. You must actively participate and function in all the district meetings.

I hope that right away you would practice speaking the Lord's word. All of you have to build up this habit. It is true that in all the meetings you need the testimonies. But to speak the Lord's word is needed more. We should also build up an atmosphere among us so that when anyone has a spiritual question, he can ask about it in the meeting. There is no need to wait until the end of the meeting to ask questions. This will encourage the mutual exhortation and encouragement. However, we should not bring these questions of the brothers and sisters outside the meetings and use them as subjects for gossip. That would give Satan a means to damage the church life.

I hope that you will all go back to practice these three things. First, pick up the burden for the meetings. If the one thousand of us go to the meetings passively, without functioning, the meetings will be through. If we learn to pick up the burden for the meetings to speak the Lord's word, the meetings will be living and rich. We have to perfect all the trainees to function in the meetings and to speak the Lord's word. However, in our functioning, we must avoid lengthy speakings. Second, not only should we speak in the meetings, but we also should speak the Lord's word in our daily life. Third, we have to encourage the brothers and sisters to bring all their questions to the meetings in order to arrive at the result of mutual encouragement. If we would practice these three things, I believe the success of the new way can be expected.

A message given by Brother Witness Lee in Taipei on October 11, 1987.

CHAPTER NINETEEN

CONCERNING SOME PRACTICAL MATTERS

This morning we want to spend some time to study further the things we should do in the present stage. At present, we have over eighty meetings in different districts in Taipei. We call them simply the "district meetings." Hence, in the present stage, we have the home meetings, the group meetings, and the district meetings.

FOUR GROUPS OF PEOPLE TAKING THE LEAD TO FUNCTION IN THE DISTRICT MEETINGS

First, we will consider the situation of the brothers and sisters, district by district. We also have to consider the distribution of the elders, the co-workers, and the full-time trainees. Then, we have to take a look at the home meetings established among the new believers in each district. According to the present arrangement, to have the church meetings and church services in the communities is a clear and accurate way. This is much more practical and suitable than the former arrangement of meeting and serving in the meeting halls.

Without Monopolizing or Replacing

For the district meetings the elders, co-workers, full-timers, and the college students should all live in the Lord's Spirit in their daily living. When these four groups of people come to the meetings, they will spontaneously have something to supply others, be able to function, and be able to speak for the Lord. What I observed here last Lord's Day was quite good. I heard that the other districts were also quite good. The elders and co-workers all spoke in the meetings, and their speaking was fresh, high, living and rich. The full-timers and the college students were equally fresh in their speaking. This is a very good situation. But I hope you will be careful not to go to either extreme of not speaking at all or speaking too much. We should not give the other brothers and sisters an impression that we are monopolizing the meeting. In Taipei the elders, co-workers, full-time trainees, and college students make up about one quarter of the total number of attendants. It would, of course, be very good if this one quarter would function. But we must also remember that our functioning is only to take the lead, and not to replace the saints. If this quarter replaces the three quarters, this will become the old system again. Formerly, it was one speaking. Now it is a group speaking. This is still not what we are after.

We can encourage the elders, co-workers, full-timers, and college students to speak one by one in the meetings. Since we are just beginning to change the system, there is the need for you to take the lead to give the brothers and sisters an example and a model to follow. However, while you are doing this, do not replace the others. I am afraid that after hearing my word, you will not function at all next week in the district meeting. That would be what the Bible describes as, "a cake not turned" (Hosea 7:8). We as the cake must be turned repeatedly. So we still should speak in the district meetings, but we should not give others the feeling, "These are the trained ones; we cannot match their speaking; we might as well let them speak." If they have such a feeling, that means we are dominating the meeting. We must guard against this danger. Therefore, I point this out from the beginning, that we are to take the lead, and not to replace others.

Standing Against the Natural Self and Sisters Keeping a Proper Position

Another thing, I have discovered is that, whether in the training meetings or in the church meetings, the young sisters are always stronger than the young brothers. I believe the main reason might be that the Bible calls the woman "the weaker, female vessel" (1 Peter 3:7). As a result, the young sisters are unwilling to be considered weak. Hence, either they will not speak at all, or they will speak impressively at the first try. Actually, there is somewhat a feeling of inferiority with them. Also, by nature, males are inferior to females in singing and speaking. Girls also speak earlier than boys do. This may be one of the reasons for the sisters' aggressiveness. Therefore, in the matter of speaking, we must stand against our natural self. Those who by nature want to speak should refrain from speaking, and those who by nature do not want to speak should speak. I am saying this to adjust you. I hope that you will not feel troubled. You must contribute your portion in a proper way.

The New Testament shows us that every woman praying or prophesying with her head uncovered disgraces her head (1 Cor. 11:5). This means that when speaking in the meetings, the sisters should not forget that they are still sisters. Some words, if spoken by brothers, will not sound strange. Even if they jump a little, that will not surprise others. But if the sisters, even though they are young, jump and speak in a wild way in the meetings, people will feel it is inappropriate. This is because in God's creation there is the distinction between male and female. I hope that the sisters would all function in the meetings. You have the riches, and these riches should be exhibited, the more the better. However, in functioning, do not forget that you are sisters.

Seizing the Opportunity to Practice Speaking for the Lord

Hebrews 10:33 says that we are "being made a spectacle." The church is a spectacle, or a show, for all to see. It is impossible to avoid criticism or praise. But I hope that we can carry out this exhibition well, and that we can meet in a proper way that will make people feel good and comfortable. Such a meeting will be an edification to people. For this, speaking in the meeting is the best opportunity to practice speaking for the Lord. I feel that the brothers and sisters should seize this opportunity, not just to shout and yell as we did formerly, but rather, to practice speaking the Lord's word. Whenever you practice speaking for the Lord in the meeting, it is best that you speak for only three minutes. At most you should not exceed five minutes. If you still have something to say, sit down first. Then speak after another one has finished speaking. In your speaking you should practice speaking in a manner that is concise, simple, and to the point. This is a good opportunity to practice. I hope that you would do your best to carry this out.

REALIZING THE IMPORTANCE
OF THE GROUP MEETING

Following this, let us take a look at the group meetings. As early as thirty years ago we realized the importance of the group meetings. The greatest usefulness of a group meeting is to bring in relatedness. A group meeting can keep people, uphold people, and relate people. No meeting can be as practical as a group meeting in communicating with and blending together the brothers and sisters. The home meetings consist basically of family members with, at most, a few friends and relatives. And the district meetings have forty to fifty people, and do not afford as much opportunity for contact. But the group meetings have at most a dozen people. The opportunity for contact is great, and all are close to one another and see one another every week. This makes it easy to have the sense of being members one of another. We all know that no member of the body can be alone or isolated. The more the members of the body fellowship and mingle together, the healthier the body will be. This is like the constant physical exercise of a man improving his blood circulation. In the same way, in the group meetings where the number is not big, the members can easily contact and fellowship with one another, and be mingled together. Once there is the mingling, many problems are solved. Human relationships are delicate. If people are too far apart, it is easy for misunderstandings to occur; but if they are too close, it is easy to have problems. The best way is to have contact, yet with discretion. The group meeting has just such a function.

In the past we already knew that to keep the saved

ones, we had to bring them into the small groups. Now in taking the new way, after three years of study, we are more clear concerning this point. From now on, our practice will consist of the home meetings on the small scale, and the district meetings on the large scale. Between the home meetings and the district meetings are the group meetings. The home meetings are the foundation. If there has not been a meeting in a brother's or sister's home for a while, this eventually will become a weak point, a leak, not only to the brother himself, but to the church as well. For the church to be strong, it is best for all the brothers and sisters to have home meetings. For the district meeting, however, we have made the decision that the basic number is fifty. Once the number exceeds eighty, it should be divided into two districts. Meanwhile, between the homes and the district must be the groups. Without the groups, there will not be any link, nor any means to uphold the brothers and sisters.

According to our experience, among the three kinds of meetings—the home meetings, the group meetings, and the district meetings—the most difficult one to have is the group meeting. The district meeting has at least thirty to forty people; it is not that difficult to take care of. But the group meeting has at most a dozen people; it is not that easy. Thirty years ago, we depended very much on the small groups. Looking back, I feel that the small groups then were not properly arranged. They were not like gardens, but rather like wild fields. Some small groups would not subdivide, even though their number reached more than a hundred. As far as I am concerned, I did not gain any experience from the former small groups. Therefore, how to have a group meeting is still a difficult problem to me. Many among you have attended three terms of training, have worked in the communities for a year and a half, and have experienced much. I would like to listen to your fellowship.

A FEW PRACTICAL QUESTIONS
CONCERNING THE GROUP MEETING

First, I would ask you how you bring people from the

home meetings to the group meetings and how you make them interested in the group meeting. Second, when they come to the group meeting, how do you conduct the meeting? In an orderly way? Or do you let it run its free course? Third, if there is a good number in the group that will not go to the district meeting, how do you help them read the Bible, pray, break bread, and even have gospel activities? After having listened to the fellowship of the brothers and sisters, I feel that the situation is very complicated. Concerning the group meeting, I still have not arrived at a conclusion. Hence, we still need to spend time to study the matter.

Another question we need to pay attention to is: when you full-time trainees go out to set up home meetings and group meetings, how do you link yourselves to the local saints? In the group meetings it is better not to distinguish between the original ones and the new ones. We are all brothers and sisters. You have to do your best to put the two groups of people together. The newly baptized ones are under your care. You know their situation very well. But the saints who have been saved and meeting in the halls for a long time do not know their situation very well, nor know how to be related to them. This requires you to bring both those who have been saved for a long time and the new ones into the same group, so that they will have more opportunities to know each other.

Moreover, when you go to conduct the group meetings, you should also consider how to bring the more experienced saints into the group meetings to share in the responsibility. Besides this, we also need to study the length of the group meetings. In the past, due to our shortage in manpower and the large number of baptisms, we could not afford to have more than half an hour for the home meetings. Now I feel that half an hour is definitely not enough for your group meetings. You cannot expect to accomplish anything in such a short time. You need at least an hour. We also need to consider how often we should have the group meetings. Should we have one a week, or one every two weeks? Also, concerning the breaking of bread, some are not willing to go to the district meeting to break bread.

Should we break bread in the home meetings or in the group meetings? All these practical questions await our study. There is another important matter that requires our study—the content of the group meetings. The key to keeping people in the group meetings is the content of the meetings. If the content is not right, the meetings will not last for long.

As to how many meetings the new ones should have each week, we must make that decision according to their condition. At present, we have three meetings each week. They are the home meeting, the group meeting, and the district meeting. Is this too much for them? Or should we be less rigid about the home meetings, not so formal, giving them the freedom to meet either in the morning or in the evening. Should we make the group meetings more fixed, and encourage them to have it once a week? This way, psychologically, they will not feel that there are too many meetings. Or, should we have the district meetings once a week, with the home meetings and group meetings being conducted alternately once every other week? All these points are worth studying.

JOINING TOGETHER
TO BEAR THE RESPONSIBILITY

At present we have made a general arrangement for all the serving ones in the different districts. We have also tabulated the number of new ones, co-workers, elders, and full-timers in each district. For example, in a certain district we may have one hundred fifty saints originally and four hundred newly baptized ones. That makes a total of five hundred fifty saints, including old and new ones. We estimate that each full-timer can take care of twenty new ones. While you are taking care of these twenty new ones, you should find a way to join the new ones with the old ones in the district. These old ones are experienced and should be brought in to coordinate with you. Their time is not so flexible as yours. The working ones have to go to their offices, and the sisters have to take care of their housework. You have to work according to their schedule and see how to put the new ones into the group. Only when these groups have been formed will there be a stable condition. All the districts should do their best to carry out these points.

Once you actually work with a group meeting, you will find many problems. For example, you may be a twenty-five year old brother. When you go out to knock on doors to preach the gospel, you may baptize a fifty-five year old college professor. After this, you may begin to have home meetings with him. Gradually, because of the difference in age, it will become difficult for the two of you to communicate with each other. Then you will need an older saint to coordinate with you for the situation. But he will have to be trained also. Otherwise, he may be able to get along well with the new one, become a friend and develop a good relationship with him, yet not render this new one much perfecting. This matter also requires our attention.

If there were not a church here in Taipei, it would be very easy in taking the new way to propagate with three or five saints to knock on doors and preach the gospel to save people. But the church in Taipei is an old church. Among the ten thousand saints here, about three thousand attend district meetings. Besides, during the past year and a half, the full-time trainees went to knock on doors to preach the gospel, and they gained over thirty thousand people. Out of these, about two thousand meet regularly, while another two to three thousand are unstable. If we add the new and the old together, we will have over eight thousand people. The urgent need is to care for them and to perfect them in the small groups. Moreover, there are still many unsettled issues concerning how to cause the useful ones to function, and how to train the ones who are not so useful to become useful. Therefore, concerning this matter, every elder, co-worker and full-time trainee must bear the responsibility.

LEARNING SERIOUSLY
AND STUDYING CONSCIENTIOUSLY

One may say that we are all learning here. I am happy

for you, because there is a rare opportunity for you to learn to serve the Lord in this environment. This will expand your horizons and enrich your experience. You can practice speaking for the Lord in the district meetings on the one hand, and learn to take care of home meetings and group meetings on the other hand. Not only do the brothers and sisters have spiritual needs, they also have psychological and physical needs. Meeting all these needs necessitates the whole church to go on together. But how to take the whole church on so that the whole church will be on the right track, how to help the saints to have a life in the Word, in prayer, and in the enjoyment of the Lord's table, as well as how to have gospel activities, these are your responsibility. The success of this matter depends totally on the carrying out of the group meetings. We will have to apply all that we have learned in these two years to the group meetings. We must spend most of our time and manpower on the home meetings and the group meetings. This does not mean that we will no longer preach the gospel. The door knocking to preach the gospel must not stop. We still need to teach new trainees how to knock on doors, to preach the gospel, and to get people baptized. We must even take out the newly saved ones to knock on doors to preach the gospel with us. When we carry out the group meetings and bring the new ones to serve, this includes the matter of knocking on doors to preach the gospel.

In conclusion, the church in Taipei is a big church. According to the present situation with the meetings, we have the home meetings, the group meetings, and the district meetings. The whole church is divided into more than eighty districts, under the twenty-three meeting halls. The meeting halls are mainly for administration, and the spiritual caring, nourishing, educating, guiding, and serving are all carried out in the districts. Hence, what we need to study the most is the matter of the various kinds of meetings. We need to do more research to find out the proper way to have the home meetings, the group meetings, and the district meetings. Meanwhile, we who are coordinating in the services, the regular serving ones in the church and the full-timers in the training, are all within the boundary of the church in Taipei. All these people are like materials piled up on a site, and not built up yet. We still do not have a definite way to coordinate them together. Therefore, we must spend time to study to find out what we lack and what we must avoid. Then, from the information gathered through experiments, we will find the proper way and apply it to the practical need of the church.

A message given by Brother Witness Lee in Taipei on November 17, 1987.

CHAPTER TWENTY

CONCERNING THE MEETINGS
IN THE NEW WAY

According to the present situation, among all the meetings of the new way, the group meeting is a very complicated one. In the group meeting there are those who have been saved for a longer time as well as the newly baptized ones; those who attend the district meetings as well as those who do not attend them; those who break bread in the homes, and those who break bread in the group meetings. The group meetings are composed of different sorts of people. Besides this, we have the goal of bringing all the students into the district meetings and even into the group meetings. At present, the church in Taipei can be compared to a large chop-suey mixing pot. Not only is the number of serving ones great; the items of services are also many. Hence, in practice, we need much of the Lord's grace that we may meet all the needs when we serve, and may be able to coordinate the serving ones from all the different areas together.

THE PRESENT SITUATION AND NEED

We all know that it is much easier to do anything if we have only one line of action. If there are many lines it will be rather difficult. We are now facing a situation with many lines. Besides those attending the district meetings, we still have over five thousand people to care for. Among them there are two thousand who were recovered from the gospel festival, and three thousand who were brought in from the door knocking during the past two years. They came from every part of society. They have meetings every week, and their condition is quite good. But they only like to meet in the homes; they do not want to come to the district meetings. From this aspect, our burden in taking care of them is too heavy. Besides this, among our trainees, we also have a very complicated situation. There are the local ones and also those from overseas. Among those from overseas, most are from America, and some are also from Southeast Asia. The lengths of the training periods they have attended are also different. Some are already in their third term, whereas some have been here only a few days. Besides this, there are the one-week trainings, the two-week trainings, the six-week trainings, the housewives' training and the older saints' training. It is very difficult to sort out all these aspects and have them in order.

The church in Taipei has been here for thirty-eight years. It surely is qualified to be called an "old church." Superficially speaking, our number is quite large. Actually, it is not large enough. Throughout the past years, according to our statistics, we have had only one hundred fifteen thousand people under our care. This is not a large number. The reason for this is that our former system of meeting was wrong. We were not able to perfect the functions within all the brothers and sisters. As a result, although our number grew larger and larger, those whose function has been truly manifested are few. This is our big lack.

RECOVERING GOD'S
NEW TESTAMENT ECONOMY

Our training here has a definite goal. This goal is to recover God's New Testament economy. The content of God's New Testament economy is that God is working Himself into a group of people, that they may become the Body of Christ as God's expression. This is the local churches in the different localities today and the New Jerusalem in the new heaven and new earth in the future as His ultimate manifestation. Although this word is simple, its content is very rich. In order for us to have a clear vision, we need to first see what kind of God our God is. Next, we need to see how He is working Himself into a group of people. Then, we want to see what kind of people are those into whom He is working Himself.

As to God, He is the Triune God. In order to work Himself into man, He needs some steps. These steps are the various processes He has gone through, which include the Father's choosing and predestinating and the Son's incarnation. When the Son came to earth, He came with the Father and by the Spirit, and lived on the earth for thirty-three and a half years. In the end He willingly went into death, gave up His soul life, was nailed to the cross, and accomplished redemption. After that, He walked into Hades and death and came out from there and entered into resurrection. In resurrection, He became the all-inclusive, life-giving Spirit. He then breathed this Spirit into those who believed in Him to become their life, their content, their supply, and everything to them. From then on, those who are chosen and called by God and who believe into Him can receive and possess Him. Not only are they regenerated; they are sanctified and transformed as well. To the Father they have become His many sons, and to the Son, His many members. In this way, the many members of the Son are constituted one Body. When this Body is expressed in the different localities, they are the local churches.

PERFECTING THE MEMBERS OF CHRIST

Now what kind of life these in the local churches should live in order to express the Body of Christ is what we want to take care of in this training. Our training is to regenerate, sanctify, and transform those who are chosen and called by God, so that they would become the Body of Christ to be expressed in the different localities. It is not a simple question as to how this group of people should live and meet in the various places to become the corporate expression of Christ. For two thousand years, Christians have not been able to understand this fully. Today, the whole of Christianity is still probing in the dark. There are few who know the direction and the goal. For this reason, we began to have this training one year ago.

NOT BEING AN UNTURNED CAKE

The first thing that this training does is to turn you

over like a cake. We all know that in baking a cake, we need to turn the cake from one side to the other repeatedly. If we do not turn the cake, the underside will be burnt while the upper side is still raw. Therefore, we need to keep turning the cake until both sides are done. Our training here is to keep you from becoming an unturned cake. Sometimes I am afraid that when we turn too hurriedly, you cannot bear it. I advise you to take these turnings because they help you to get rid of your old concepts and ways and to deliver you from your old background and habits. Every one of us has three layers of inheritance from tradition. The first layer comes with our birth. Although we were created by God, we were born fallen. Whether we are Chinese, American, or Japanese, we were born into Adam's race. We all have many problems with our character: laziness, sloppiness, and looseness. These are our nature. The second layer comes from the tradition in Christianity. We were born into human society. Because Christianity came to the East along with western culture, we have more or less been influenced by the traditions in Christianity. The third layer comes from the practices among us that have been inherited from Christianity. All these three layers, whatever they are, are not scriptural. More or less, they have been utilized by Satan to annul what God is doing and what He is going to gain in man.

CHRISTIANITY ANNULLING THE FUNCTION OF THE MEMBERS OF THE BODY OF CHRIST

We have said that God's economy is to work Himself into a group of people that they may be regenerated, sanctified, and transformed, so that they may become the sons of God and the members of Christ to be constituted as the Body of Christ. If we compare every point of this vision with the practices of today's Christianity, we will realize that the practices of Christianity have either reduced or annulled these points. For example, a person hears the gospel and is saved. After he is saved, he does not need anyone to tell him, but spontaneously he has the concept to do good, to worship God, to attend Sunday services, to listen to the pastor's preaching, and to learn doctrines. He will join a congregation and become a church member, and come to attend services every Sunday. This can go on for twenty or thirty years, and eventually he becomes an old Christian. As far as God's economy is concerned, although he is regenerated, there is no sanctification expressed in him, nor is there any transformation, much less any functioning. His organic function in the Body of Christ is altogether annulled. There are many believers among the different denominations in Christianity who are all chosen, redeemed, and regenerated by God. But their life function is completely annulled by the practices of traditional religion. We do not see much sanctification and transformation in them, nor do we recognize in their daily walk the mark of the sons of God. Furthermore, we could not see that they are the members of the Body of Christ to be constituted as the Body of Christ. On the contrary, we only see some religious formalities and worship activities.

Among us, although we have left degraded Christianity to come into the Lord's recovery, it is not easy to stay in the recovery. I am afraid that our real situation has been gradually declining. This was especially true at the end of 1984 when I came back to Taiwan. There were brothers and sisters meeting everywhere. Few came prepared to function; rather, most of them came with a mentality to listen to messages. The responsible brothers in all the meeting halls tried their best to arrange for speakers to release messages week after week. Our practice was still to have those that came to the meetings sit there and listen to one man speaking. It is true that the messages did render people some help. But this help eventually made people dumb in speaking and paralyzed in their function.

In the old practice, the more the people listen to messages, the more they like to listen, and the less they function. When a person is first saved, he may still want to give testimonies in the meetings. But due to the atmosphere of the meetings, gradually the speaking function is annulled. This practice nullifies the life of the Son of God in the believers, and buries the organic function in the members of Christ. After the brothers and sisters are accustomed to listening to messages, they become settled. As a result, the condition of the whole church is stagnant; there are not many positive activities taking place. It is like a man over sixty years of age, lacking youthful vitality. Although the brothers and sisters still love the Lord and love the church; and although they still stand on the ground, learning to live in the spirit, and are neither backsliding nor cold, yet there is no more drive. They are not like a youth of eighteen or nineteen years old, full of vitality and vigor. On the contrary, they are half-dead, like the situation in Christianity.

BACK TO THE WAY OF MEETING
REVEALED IN THE BIBLE

I have been exploring the situation among us. Generally speaking, the brothers and sisters are all very good; especially those who are stable are quite seeking. But why is there a condition of stagnation? The reason is that our system of meeting and service is wrong. This is why I have come back to the Bible again to look at this matter. The meetings spoken of in the Bible are occasions for people to be encouraged, to be stirred up, to speak, and to function (1 Cor. 14:24-25, 31). When you want to speak in the meetings, you may discover that your personal condition is not right. Hence, you must seek for a revival; you must pray, confess, and consecrate yourself to God, and you must adjust your spiritual life so that you would have a new beginning before the Lord. You will see that although you are in the Lord's recovery, yet your family life is loose and sloppy, and your spirit is not strong and aggressive. Therefore, you will not be able to function in the meeting. For this reason you must live an overcoming life every day.

Brothers and sisters, please remember that the way of meeting as revealed in the Bible is one that enlivens people. It revives man's spirit and develops the organic function in man. It develops from within man the initial gift received from God. This initial gift is the divine life of God, which is capable of growing within us in the same way that the life within a baby will grow. When this life grows, the functions of life are developed from within the baby gradually, causing the baby to see, to hear, to speak, to work with his hands, and to walk with his feet. However, the system of meeting in today's Christianity does not develop the spiritual function of life within us, the regenerated ones. On the contrary, it restricts, limits, and suppresses our spiritual functions, with the result that they are reduced or annulled.

The way to meet as revealed in the Bible establishes and builds up the function of life in us, and it stirs up all the gifts of the divine life that the saints received from God; the result will be that they are nourished and supplied. By this the saints grow, and the growth of the saints is the building up of the church. However, I have seen some brothers and sisters among us who come to every meeting, who participate in all the services, who are very faithful in listening to messages, and who love the Lord; yet, we do not see much growth in life in them. The reason is that there is not much supply and nourishment in the meetings, and also there is the lack of the release and exercise of life. For this reason, in the meetings under the old system, it is difficult to see any growth in life, and there is very little building.

All of you as trainees must understand that this training is to bring us back to the way of meeting as revealed in the Bible. By this the saints will be supplied and nourished in the meetings, and they will have the opportunity to exercise and to develop their functions. As long as the saints are supplied and nourished in a timely way, and as long as they have the proper exercise and development, the life in them will spontaneously grow. The result will be building. This building, strictly speaking, is not individual but corporate, for it is in the meetings that we are built up together. In other words, as we grow together in the church, the Body will be built up. Individually speaking, we grow by being nourished and exercised in the spiritual life; corporately speaking, we are built up in the Body. By this, the testimony of the Body of Christ will be manifested.

THE MEETINGS' REQUIREMENTS
FOR THE SAINTS IN THE NEW WAY

We all must see that the development of the organic ability and function within the saints is the most crucial item of the way to meet as revealed in the Bible. In the process of this development of their organic ability, the activities of the brothers and sisters may not be on the right track. But we should not limit them too much, neither should we be too restrictive. The less we restrict and limit them, the more they will have the development. When their functions are developed, we can then guide them into the proper way to function. Then their activities in the meetings will be proper.

The way to meet as revealed in the Bible requires us to do three things. First, we must be revived. In order to have a revival, we must live daily in the Spirit, walk by the Spirit, and conduct ourselves according to the Spirit. Only then will we be able to have any activity in the way of meeting as revealed in the Bible. Our activity is based on our being living, and this livingness is not a performance. Rather, it is the result of our fellowship with the Lord in our daily life. Formerly, in the old way, even though we might have been dead for years and might not have prayed for three months, we could still come to the meetings. However, in the new way, you cannot afford to be out of the spirit for even half a day, not to say a whole day. If you had a good morning but were out of the spirit in that afternoon, you would feel inadequate when you come to the meeting in the evening. Hence, the new way requires that we be spiritual and that we live in the spirit all day long. The success of the new way does not depend on how much we know the techniques, and it does not depend on us teaching others about the Word, the Spirit, singing, and prayer. Rather, it depends on us being a living person before the Lord, one who lives in the spirit. Second, we must enjoy the Lord's word. The Lord has given us not only the Holy Spirit within, but also the Bible without. The Bible is a wonderful book that enables us to enjoy the Lord. Therefore, we must learn to enjoy the word of the Lord daily. If our spirit is living, and we have the Lord's word, then we can learn to sing and pray. This is not an outward method. Rather, it is a matter of being living, of living in the spirit, fellowshipping with the Lord, and enjoying the Lord's word constantly. Third, if we are this kind of person, surely we will love to go to meetings. In the meetings, we will be able to function freely. Whether it is a home meeting, a group meeting, or a district meeting, we will be able to meet the needs of others.

Our training here is not to teach you a method. Neither are you here to learn any new methods to take back to your locality. That is worthless. If you do this, it is not "the new man walking the new way." Rather, it is the dead man changing the coffin. The goal of our training is to enliven the old man that he may become the new man to function in the meetings. As long as the saints would supply life by functioning in the meetings, the result will be the growth of life and the building up together. Furthermore, the individual building up will issue in the building up of the Body.

EVERYONE REVIVED TO DEVELOP
THE ORGANIC FUNCTION

I hope these words will give you a deep impression that you will have a new beginning and be revived from within: those who did not taste the Lord before will now be able to taste the Lord, those who did not enter into the Lord's words before can now enter in. In this way, your spirit will be strong, and you will be rich in the enjoyment of the Lord's word. Then when you come to the meetings, you will speak the Lord's word. Strictly speaking, the Lord's word does not start in the meeting. It starts from the time you wake up in the morning. You should speak to the Lord, and you should pray-read the word of the Lord. By the time you go to work and meet your colleagues, or when you go to school and meet your classmates, you should speak the word of the Lord at any time. During the day, whenever you meet someone, you should speak the word of the Lord. Do this until the evening when you come to the meeting.

If you are such a person, then whether you go to the home meeting, the group meeting, or the district meeting, you will be a supplier. You will always be one that nourishes others. Actually, when you nourish others, you will be the first one to be nourished. In a meeting, the first one to be nourished is always the speaker. If you do not speak, you are depriving yourself of any nourishment. The minute you speak, you nourish yourself, and you nourish others. As a result, all the saints nourish one another and are nourished by one another. This kind of meeting brings out the riches of the Lord's life in us, just as those digging gold from the mine. Such meetings also develop the organic ability and function within each one.

This morning I am like a crowing rooster. I am giving all of you trainees a warning. First, I hope that you would change your concepts and would have a full understanding of the new way. Do not go to the home meetings or group meetings with the thought that you have seniority. You must be renewed continually. Every day you should be living and fresh. Then, when you go to work, you should forget about the old ways. Do not ask what the new method is, for it is not a matter of the method, but of the person, whether or not your person is living. Within us, we all have the vigorous life of the Lord, which is the Triune God. Also, we have a living Bible in our hands. As long as our spirits are living and bubbling, and as long as we enjoy the Triune God through the Bible daily, we will surely be able to practice the new way.

A message given by Brother Witness Lee in Taipei on November 19, 1987.

Chapter Twenty-One

CONCERNING THE PRACTICE OF GROUP MEETINGS

This morning we will study the way to take care of small groups. Since October of 1984 when we first mentioned the change of the system, we have been practicing small group meetings here in Taipei. At that time, we had a slogan: "The heaven can be annulled, and the earth can pass away, but the small group meeting must not be forsaken." Afterwards, we were divided into four hundred small groups, and the number of attendants was between three thousand and thirty-five hundred. After promoting these groups for more than a year, from 1985 to the spring of 1986, the number of attendants in the small group meetings rose to over five thousand. From this we can see the effectiveness of small groups.

BRINGING THE NEW ONES TO THE EXISTING SMALL GROUPS

In the second half of 1986, we began to conduct formal trainings, and we tried our best to bring the local saints into those trainings. At that time there were over a thousand saints who had attended the evening trainings at various times. Most of these were the nucleus of the church in Taipei. The four hundred small groups were on their shoulders. As soon as they came forward to attend the training, the small groups were left untended. As a result, during the last year, although the small groups still existed, they were in a situation where they were left to themselves.

In spite of this, these first small groups are still a foundation. They are still quite useful. At present in the church in Taipei there are about thirty-five hundred saints who attend meetings regularly in the halls. The number of those who were brought in through gospel preaching by door knocking in the communities and who have meetings every week is about two thousand. The two groups comprise more than six thousand people. It is not much of a problem for those who have been meeting in the halls to come to the group meetings or district meetings, because they are accustomed to them already. However, of the two thousand new ones, only seven to eight hundred are willing to go to the district meetings; the rest are not willing to leave their homes to meet in other places. Under these circumstances, we cannot expect these new ones to raise up small groups within a short time. Therefore, we still need to take those who originally attended the meetings in the halls as a foundation. By making a new arrangement for these small groups, we can gradually bring the new ones into them.

Today, the housing situation in Taipei is very different from what it used to be. In the old days, we mostly had single houses clearly separated from one another. But now, we have large apartment buildings within which are many dwelling units. When we have meetings with singing and praying in the homes, it is difficult not to disturb the neighbors. Hence, it is not easy to open up a new place for meeting. In addition, it is also quite difficult to ask the new ones to willingly open up their homes to have group meetings week after week. Therefore, a meeting place for the small groups also becomes a problem. As for the original four hundred groups, because they had been established a long time ago, the neighbors are more accustomed to the noise of our meetings. For this reason, we still need to utilize the original groups. However, it does not mean that we should never set up new small groups in the communities. If our newly baptized ones live far away from the existing groups, or if there is not a group that is suitable for them, it would not be easy to bring them to the group meetings. In such cases, we have to open up new small groups for them. This matter is related to the exercise and practice in our training. When you go to take care of home meetings and from the home meetings develop small group meetings, you need to consider the practical situation. For those living in remote places, there is the need to establish new small groups. It is not necessary for the training center to promote this, nor is it necessary for the elders or the district leaders to arrange for this. You workers need to make the decision according to the practical situation.

After the change of the system, our principle is freedom of development. Since you are the ones taking care of the home meetings in a practical way, and you understand their actual situation, you can work according to the practical needs. If the new ones live far away from the original small groups and it becomes difficult for them to attend, you need to set up new small groups for them. If their situation is not appropriate, and if no one has picked up the burden to start a new group, you need to help them travel a little farther to go to the most suitable place to attend group meetings. They can see the meeting for themselves and have a taste. In this way, they will be raised up gradually and will have the desire to establish small groups.

THE CONTENT OF GROUP MEETINGS

With Humanity and Avoiding Leaven

Now let us consider the content of group meetings. Although in 1986 the number in the small groups increased from three thousand to over five thousand with an increase rate of seventy-five percent, the content of our group meetings has never been uplifted. Our past method was simply to have some refreshments and some casual talk. These activities occupied a large portion of the time. Although it is difficult to avoid having casual talk, I would like you to do your best to avoid this. However, you should not avoid it to the extent that your behavior is as cold and stiff as a piece of rock or a piece of steel when you go to meet in others' homes. You can be assured that this will not work. We are human, and no human being can be without warmth. As long as we are living persons, we have humanity. Only a dead person would fail to greet others or smile at them. We, however, are living persons, and sometimes we would even smile at cats and dogs. Therefore, we always need to remember that we are going to contact people; since this is the case, we need to do it with a humanity that is adequate.

Christianity has been on the earth for almost two thousand years. Their way of gaining people in general is through preaching, on the one hand, and through the use of other things, on the other hand. These other things are the leaven hidden in the fine flour, as mentioned in Matthew 13:33. In the Old Testament, the fine flour is for the meal offering (Lev. 2:1), and the meal offering signifies Christ as food for both God and man. Concerning the meal offering, God has a strict ordinance that no leaven is allowed. In conjunction with this, things that will ferment, such as honey, are also not allowed (Lev. 2:4-5, 11). Only salt is allowed in the fine flour, because salt kills germs. In Matthew 13, the Lord Jesus likens Himself to the fine flour, whereas the woman is the great harlot in Revelation 17, who is the Roman Catholic Church. She has mixed the pagan practices, heretical doctrines, and evil things into the teachings concerning Christ, and thus changed the nature of their content. In all of the works of Christianity today, there is not much that is without leaven. For example, in the Chinese Christian work in the United States, the thing most commonly seen is social friendship, which is something of leaven. Their workers only render help to people outwardly; they do not bring people into Christ, nor do they bring Christ into people. The messages given do not have much truth, and they gain people mostly through social activities. I am afraid that about eighty percent of those attending their meetings are there for social friendship.

Rendering Help to People for the Dispensing of the Triune God into Them

Apparently, Christianity has brought in many people. Actually, their gain is not that large because those who go to them are mostly there for some outward help. This is like what the Lord Jesus said in John 6, "You seek

Me...because you ate of the bread and were satisfied"
(v. 26). They did not desire the Lord or seek after Him in a
genuine way. The situation today is the same. There are,
indeed, many hardships in human life. However, when you
go to help the new ones, you need to weigh carefully how
much outward help you should render to them. You should
not think that as long as you do your best to help others, it
will be effective. You have to realize that there is no end to
people's demand for help. Therefore, we need to set a limit
to this kind of thing, and the limit should depend on the
circumstance. If we cannot bring a person into Christ in a
practical way, though we have tried our best, we simply
have to put this one aside temporarily. We cannot spend all
of our effort only to care for this kind of person.

Therefore, when you go out, you should not be bothered
too much by these things. On the one hand, you should not
be cold and stiff toward people; you always need to cause
people to feel warm. On the other hand, you should not be
snared by this; otherwise, you will not be able to do anything else. This is something that we have been guarding
against for years. It is not that we have no heart to help
others, but sometimes we do not dare to do too much. This
is the principle of the Lord Jesus. When the crowd who had
been fed with bread came to force Him to be king, He
retreated to the mountains, Himself alone. The next day
they looked all around for the Lord Jesus. Later they found
Him by the sea. Then the Lord told them that the Son of
Man came not to feed people with bread, but to dispense
Himself as the bread of life into men (John 6:24-27). What
He did the day before was merely a symbolic act to show
people that they are hungry and that He is the bread that
came down from heaven to give life to man.

In the same principle, it is not that today we do not care
for people; rather, we care for people within a limit. Most
people consider the church as a charitable organization
with a goal of seeking the welfare of the society. You
cannot say that this is absolutely wrong, but this is not the
commission we received from God. The commission that
we have received from God is to dispense the Triune God

into people to be everything to them. This, then, is the real blessing to man. We must hold on to this point firmly.

Flexible in Application, Quick in Response

Concerning the content of group meetings, I would say that in principle we should have freedom for development. When you take care of a group meeting, you need to consider the practical environment and the need. The purpose of our training is to train you to be quick in response and to supply people according to their need. You should not pick up only one prescription and try to apply it to all sick people. You need to be able to diagnose people to identify their needs. This is why you have much to learn. When a new small group is raised up, or when an existing small group has a new beginning, the brothers and sisters in the group should first have some simple fellowship concerning when each one was saved, how each one is doing, and what needs or problems each one has. After you understand the situation, then you can do your best to supply each one according to the needs. This is one way. Besides this, you may share in the meeting in a spontaneous way what you have enjoyed in fellowshipping with the Lord and reading the Lord's word recently. At the same time, you can fellowship with those serving together and check the feeling of each one concerning whether to use the *Truth Lessons* or the *Life Lessons*. You do not have to be so legal to start from Lesson One. You can select one topic or one lesson according to the need and then labor together. You can also use other spiritual publications. The New Testament Recovery Version will soon be published in Chinese and made available. By then, you can use that also. While you are using these materials, you should not forget that the basic principle of the group meetings is the Word, the Spirit, singing, and praying. You must conduct the meetings according to this principle.

BEING FLEXIBLE CONCERNING THE DATE, THE TIME, AND THE PERSONS FOR THE SMALL GROUP MEETINGS

In carrying out the group meetings, we should put all

the elders, co-workers, full-timers, and trainees into the groups. In 1985 and 1986, when we were working on the small groups, not many elders participated. Even the co-workers felt not to be involved. I hope this time that the elders would all attend the group meetings. The co-workers should not be an exception. All the other trainees, especially the full-timers, are required to attend. You are the definite members of the small groups. Hence, the group meetings cannot be all on the same day of the week. Formerly, the group meetings of the church in Taipei were all on Saturday evenings. If someone attended one group, he could not attend another group. This time, we will not set a day for the group meeting. During the week we can have group meetings at various times. If you have the burden, you can attend two or more group meetings. Not only are we flexible about the day, we should be flexible about the time as well, not all meeting at 7:30. Some groups can meet at 6:30 in the evening. Some can meet at 7:30. Some have to meet at 8:30. Due to late working hours, some can even meet at 10:30. The time and the date can be arranged individually. Therefore, you can come to my group and I can attend your group. In this way, there can be flexibility in the use of personnel. Hence, this time I do not agree with any legal arrangement concerning the date, the time, and the persons for the group meetings. Rather, those taking care of the small groups should be free to make their own decisions.

LEARNING TO LIVE
AMONG THE BROTHERS AND SISTERS

Now, in Taipei, you full-timers are mainly those taking care of the small groups. You have a few hundred in number and all of you need to enter into the small groups. In the future, the group meetings will be mainly led by you. Leading these groups is much more complicated than what you have learned in the trainings you have received before. I hope that this aspect can be taken more into consideration in this training to give you some guidance. For example, in the existing small groups, there are two kinds of older people. One kind is those who are old spiritually. The other is those who are old physically. You will have to learn much about how to fellowship with them and develop their organic function. Some do not regard young people. These problems related to age differences are unavoidable. When you young ones attend the group meetings with older ones, you need to learn not to have feelings towards such situations. Remember that your status is different from that of the others. They can speak lightly concerning this and that, but you are there with a commission. You have forsaken everything to serve full-time on this line. You go to the group meetings with a purpose. No matter what others think of you, you have to exert your whole strength to reach your goal, and not stop short. However, you should not be rigid and unbending either. Here are many details that you need a lot of time to learn.

In addition, there may be another kind of atmosphere in the small group. Some who are your age may not be cooperative. They wait to see what you can do and what you will do. In this atmosphere, you have to imitate the feeling of the Lord Jesus when He was on the cross. He knew that His going to the cross was to die for sinners and to accomplish God's redemption. You have to realize that to go to the group meeting is simply to go to the cross. Especially you young full-time trainees have to be prepared to be crucified.

There is also another group of people in the small groups, the middle-aged sisters. They are very discerning and observant. They want to see how you trainees speak, what you wear, and how you respond. This is like the Lord Jesus being examined by the Pharisees and the Sadducees a few days before His crucifixion. When you go to the small groups, you have to be prepared to be examined by others. When I first came out to serve the Lord, I was about your age. I have tasted all these things, and I know all these stories. We who are working for the Lord are really under the observations of a thousand eyes and have a thousand fingers pointing at us. Whatever we do, others would have something to say. Nevertheless, you young ones should not let others despise your youth; rather, in every respect let your progress be manifest to all.

LESSONS TO BE LEARNED
BY THE FULL-TIME SERVING ONES

Learning Not to React
to Others' Criticisms and Their Treatment

This is a training. I would like to present all the situations to you, so that you will know where you are, what you are doing, and what your goal is. We who serve the Lord must learn the lesson not to react to any outward circumstances. You must not react to the dealing of the older ones. You must not react to the dealing of those of your own age. You must not react to the dealing of the middle-aged sisters. No matter who is dealing with you and in what aspect, your secret is not to react. When the Lord Jesus was on earth, He was like a deaf person, not hearing the slandering of man and not reacting to slandering words. If you react, you will be affected, and your small group will not be able to meet after a few times.

We who serve the Lord would all like to be welcomed. We hope others would be nice to us and honor us. The real situation, however, is exactly the opposite. Before you were serving the Lord, others may have considered you to be quite good. Once you serve the Lord, others will have a lot of criticisms about you. Psychologically, the brothers and sisters may admire you for giving up your future and consecrating everything to the Lord at such a young age, yet on the other hand they would scrutinize you to see how you do. The best thing to do at this time is not to react, but to be deaf and blind. Do not react when others treat you well. Do not react when others treat you poorly. Do not react when others exalt you, and do not react when others trample you under their feet. The first lesson for us full-time serving ones is not to react.

Learning to Supply Others with Life and Truth,
and Learning to Receive Others' Supply

The second lesson we need to learn is to supply others.

We need to supply others with truth and life. In brief, we need to supply others with Christ. Whether we are attending the group meetings, the home meetings, or the district meetings, we have to do this. The Apostle Paul served the Lord according to this principle: it was not his concern to be welcomed by others or to be exalted by them. Therefore, he did not care about others' contempt or indifference. His heart had only one desire: to supply others with Christ and to receive a supply from them. We who are serving the Lord today should be the same. You go to the meetings to supply others and to be supplied by them. You should receive from whoever can supply you, no matter who he is. If you do this, the group meetings will surely be successful. The older saints, the younger saints, and the middle-aged sisters will all receive a supply from you. You must learn this.

Taking Heed to One's Own Words and Conduct

Now let me come back to point out your shortcomings and weaknesses. When you young people speak, often you do not consider your own status and position. When you hear something from me, you go out and speak the same thing. As a result, many times you cause trouble. This is because you are not I. Moreover, my words are spoken with various considerations. Sometimes it is also difficult for me to give a message. I am a straightforward person. Some words I need to say. But when you young ones hear them, you go out and repeat them. This is very inappropriate. You need to know that the church in Taipei is a large church today. There are all kinds of people here. We need to be careful about our words and our conduct. As to a rebuke from the brothers and sisters, the best way to handle it is not to react. At the same time, we need to learn more, pray more, contact the Lord and have fellowship with Him more. We need to give more ground to the Spirit that we may be filled with Him; for only in the Spirit is there the death of Christ, the resurrection of Christ, and the wisdom of Christ. I hope that these things would become your practice during the time of your training. Take care of the home meetings, and at the same time practice these things.

Keeping the Oneness of the Body of Christ

I have also heard that with some teams, the members cannot coordinate together. If the members of the same team cannot coordinate together, how can you take care of the groups? This time, our arrangement of the groups includes all the elders, co-workers, full-timers, and trainees. The majority of your work as full-timers is to care for the home meetings with a view to the group meetings. Therefore, you will encounter all the lessons that I have just mentioned. What each group should do, and what materials should be used in the meetings are details that can be left to the fellowship of the leading ones in the district meetings. When you leading ones come together, surely there will be opinions. It is not easy for all to be in one accord. Here are many lessons that are hard to learn. But we have the Lord, the killing of the cross, and the resurrection life. By these we can keep the oneness of the Body of Christ. In this oneness, we can live and work together.

A message given by Brother Witness Lee in Taipei on November 19, 1987.

CHAPTER TWENTY-TWO

TAKING IN THE LORD'S WORD AND BEING EXERCISED IN IT

Scripture Reading: Col. 3:16; Heb. 5:13-14

This morning, we come to the matter of speaking in the meetings. We have said before that the meeting God desires is one in which all the believers can speak. The focus of a meeting is its speaking. In a meeting, if there is speaking which is proper, good, living, and rich, the meeting will be proper.

EVERYONE SPEAKING THE LORD'S WORD MAKING THE MEETING ENJOYABLE

Christianity has degraded to today's fallen condition because few people are able to speak the Lord's word in the meetings. At the time of the worship service, only the pastor who has been trained in speaking speaks. All the rest just listen in silence. This is because they cannot speak and have nothing to say. This is the situation of the worship service in all of Christianity. In the Lord's recovery, our meetings in general have also fallen into the same condition of not speaking. We only have a little speaking in the bread-breaking meeting. Actually, that cannot be considered as speaking the Lord's word; there are merely some prayers and praises. Yet to everyone's feeling, the most enjoyable and the best meeting is this bread-breaking meeting. This is because in the bread-breaking meeting everyone practices speaking some words of praise. When everyone speaks, the meeting is certainly attractive. In the early days, the words of praise spoken by the brothers and sisters in the bread-breaking meetings were quite simple. Yet the meetings were still very enjoyable. But after a while, the words of praise became monotonous; and eventually, no one had much feeling about those words any more. By 1961, we added some new songs and published some messages on God's economy. After that, the praises in the bread-breaking meeting had more depth of content and the meeting became more enjoyable. For example, *Hymns*, #203, verse 3 says:

> Once Thou wast the only grain, Lord,
>   Falling to the earth to die,
> That thru death and resurrection
>   Thou in life may multiply.
> We were brought forth in Thy nature
>   And the many grains became;
> As one loaf we all are blended,
>   All Thy fulness to proclaim.

Singing and speaking the above words in the bread-breaking meeting truly touches the burden and feeling in our spirit. It makes the meeting more enjoyable and more nourishing.

THE DEVELOPMENT OF HYMNS
IN THE LORD'S RECOVERY

I would like to speak briefly concerning our hymnal. The first stage began over sixty years ago when we were raised up by the Lord. The hymnals used by Christianity at that time were not suitable for the saints' use in the Lord's recovery. We read of the hymnals published by the Brethren during their golden age. Brother Nee borrowed the table of contents of their hymnals as the basic structure for ours and added two more topics related to the spiritual warfare and the subjective experience of the cross. These were compiled into a hymnal. This hymnal begins with praises to the Father for our worship of the Father. There was also the appreciation of the Lord for our remembrance of the Lord. This rendered great help to the bread-breaking meetings. At that time, our hymnal only had one hundred eighty-three hymns and we used it until we came to Taiwan. In 1949, the young people's work began in Taiwan. We felt that the one hundred eighty-three hymns were not adequate, so we published a second volume of our hymnal. By 1961, we began to see God's economy. I wrote eighty-five hymns which became the so-called "Supplement of 85 Hymns." They were all related to God's economy and included such hymns as "Thou Art All My Life, Lord," "O Glorious Christ, Savior Mine," and "The Spirit Begets the Spirit, The Spirit Worships the Spirit" [not available in English]. In 1967, after I finished the compilation of the English hymnal in America, I returned to Taiwan and combined the two volumes of the Chinese hymnal, the "Supplement of 85 Hymns," and the gospel songs into a single volume. In addition, I added two hundred more hymns. The result is the Chinese hymnal that we are using today.

When this new hymnal was published, the brothers and sisters did not know how to appreciate it very much. As a result, when they broke bread to remember the Lord, they still selected the old hymns that they were accustomed to. Because we published many messages to promote God's economy, the brothers and sisters were gradually brought into this new flow during the last twenty years. They began to love these hymns. For example, *Hymns*, #203 says:

> In the bosom of the Father,
>   Ere the ages had begun,
> Thou wast in the Father's glory,
>   God's unique begotten Son.
> When to us the Father gave Thee,
>   Thou in person wast the same,
> All the fulness of the Father
>   In the Spirit to proclaim.
>
> By Thy death and resurrection,
>   Thou wast made God's firstborn Son;
> By Thy life to us imparting,
>   Was Thy duplication done.
> We, in Thee regenerated,
>   Many sons to God became;
> Truly as Thy many brethren,
>   We are as Thyself the same.

Just singing the above hymn will bring us into God's economy. If you go back to the hymns written by the

Brethren, they will no longer be that enjoyable. Take, for example, *Hymns*, #226:

> For the bread and for the wine,
> For the pledge that seals Him mine,
> For the words of love divine,
> We give Thee thanks, O Lord.

This is a very good hymn among the Brethren for the remembrance of the Lord. Brother Nee's translation into Chinese was also excellent. But the content of the hymn is merely a gratitude and remembrance concerning the Lord's death, sacrifice, and the shedding of His blood. It does not have much to do with God's economy. Their knowledge and experience of the Lord's word during that period only went that far. Accordingly, their feelings expressed in their hymns went only that deep. Among their hymns or books you cannot find anything like:

> O glorious Christ, Savior mine,
> Thou art truly radiance divine,
> God infinite, in eternity,
> Yet man in time, finite to be.
>   (*Hymns*, #501)

Because they did not have this kind of knowledge nor this kind of feeling, they could not have this kind of expression.

LETTING THE WORD OF CHRIST DWELL IN US

I mentioned at the beginning that the key to meeting is speaking. When the Brethren were raised up by the Lord, their influence was mainly due to their speaking. During that period, although their understanding and experience were only up to a certain level, the power of their speaking was like dynamite. Brother Nee once said that during that period their revelation and light were like the pouring down of a waterfall. D. M. Panton also said that the strength of the Brethren movement was greater than that of the Reformation by Luther. However, we feel that the Lord is always going on. In every age, He has a leading for

that age. As far as we are concerned, since 1949, I have
had no more burden to preach the things of the Brethren
period. All that I wrote were words concerning God's
economy, such as:

> O what a miracle, my Lord,
> That I'm in Thee and Thou in me,
> That Thou and I are really one;
> O what a wondrous mystery!
> (*Hymns*, #233)

Today we have changed the system. The revelation and
light that the Lord has given us have advanced even more.
We need to return to the Bible to recover the meeting
revealed in 1 Corinthians 14, where the secret is altogether
in speaking. Whether the Lord can have a way among us
depends fully on our attitude towards the Lord's word.
Some have memorized the Scriptures thoroughly, but they
cannot speak the Lord's word. This is because they have
not allowed the Lord's word to enter into them and to
occupy them. Colossians 3:16 says, "Let the word of Christ
dwell in you richly, in all wisdom." The Chinese Union
Version translated the word "dwell" as "be kept." This is
similar to a man returning from the market with a lot of
rice, flour, vegetables, meat, and all kinds of food yet
merely keeping them; these foods are not related to the
buyer of these goods. Some may have memorized a lot of
Scriptures. But these Scriptures are just kept there, and
have nothing to do with the one who memorized them. But
what Paul meant is that the Lord's word is a living Person.
In other words, the Lord's word is the Lord Himself. Hence,
we have to let Him dwell in us. The word "let" is very
meaningful. It is like our knocking on doors to preach the
gospel. On the one hand, we like to go in; on the other
hand, the ones behind the door have to let us in. Many
times we have locked our doors tight and would not let the
Lord come in. But as soon as we would give a crack for the
Lord's word, the Lord would come in.

The word "dwell" here in Greek has the sense of being
at home, indwelling, and abiding. It has the same root as

the word "make home" in Ephesians 3:17. This means that the Lord's word must have full ground in us in order to operate and supply the riches of Christ to our inner man. To let the word of Christ dwell in us is different from providing hospitality to a guest for three to five days. Instead, it is like someone moving into a new house, settling down, and making home there. Every corner of this house is for his use and control. Only this can be considered as making home. When the Lord's word enters into us, it must make home in us this way. We should let the Lord's word be our Master, taking ground in us, occupying us, so that it can move freely in us. When you allow this living word, this living Person, to abide in you, to fill and occupy your whole being, and to move freely in you, you are taking in the Lord's word. Some people have problems with their digestive systems; their stomachs are so damaged that nothing eaten can be digested. Whatever they eat is completely excreted. Although they eat food, the food does not have much to do with them. It is not digested and absorbed by them to become their elements. Hence, not only do we have to learn to receive the Lord's word into us; we have to allow the word received to occupy a place in us, to be digested into us, to be one with us, and even to become our elements.

Many of you are memorizing two verses every morning. This is a good practice. But I am afraid after you have memorized dozens of verses, you still have nothing to speak in the meeting. Even though you have the words of the Bible, they cannot become the words out of your mouth because you have not digested and absorbed them. I hope that the words that we speak in the meetings are the words taken in and digested by us. For this, we must allow the word to rule, to occupy the proper place, and to operate freely in us, so that we would be fully taken over by it to become one with it. The word is the Lord Himself, and the Lord is the Spirit. Therefore, this word is the Spirit. In our experience it is very difficult to separate the word from the Spirit. In other words, when we receive the Lord's word into us, this word becomes the Spirit. When this Spirit is spoken out from within us, it becomes the word. The Bible without is the Lord's word; when we receive it into us, it becomes the Spirit. When the Spirit is expressed from within us, it becomes the word again. The word becomes the Spirit, and the Spirit becomes the word. By this cycling, the word will spontaneously become a part of your being. In this way, it will be very easy to speak when you come to the meeting.

Hence, not only do you have to practice speaking in the meetings, you must also in your daily life let the Lord's word, which is a living Person, gain the ground in you, operate in you, and act freely in you. When you are one with the word, it will become the words that you can speak. This is like a person who after enjoying some beautiful scenery, has the view impressed into him, and upon returning, spontaneously has a lot to say. You full-timers have, so to speak, your own line of business. Your line of business is speaking. This is why we have to do our best to exercise ourselves in the enjoyment, experience, expression, and release of the Lord's word.

THE WAY FOR CHRISTIANS TO MEET BEING A WAY OF REVIVAL AND OVERCOMING

We have seen that the way for Christians to meet as revealed in the Bible is a way of revival and overcoming. If we are not revived and overcoming, and if we do not live in the spirit, then we will be through. If we want to walk properly in this way, we must be ones who are overcoming, spiritual, living in the spirit, and fellowshipping with the Lord. Not only so, we hope that we can influence all the brothers and sisters so that everyone would be revived. If we would be faithful to carry out this new way of the Lord perfectly, the result will be a great revival. If there are ten attending a meeting, all ten will be revived. If a hundred are meeting, all one hundred will be revived. If a thousand are meeting, all one thousand will be revived. Wherever there is a meeting, there will be a revival. This is a tremendous thing! Today there are hundreds of millions of Christians on the earth, yet Christianity is completely powerless. This is because the old way of meeting in Christianity has annulled the function of so many. Since we in the Lord's recovery want to return to the Bible to take the way of life, we can no longer expect to have this kind of preaching meeting with one speaking and the rest listening. Every one of us must exercise to practice speaking the Lord's word. Not only the brothers have to practice this; the sisters have to practice this as well. I hope that in your four months' training here, you would specifically practice speaking. Of course, you still have to take care of the home meetings and bring people to the group meetings. The key now is how you speak the Lord's word.

APPLYING THE LORD'S WORD
BY TAKING IT IN AND BEING EXERCISED IN IT

In order to speak in the meeting, it is not enough just to memorize a few verses of the Bible, nor will we succeed just by practicing for eight or ten days. You must spend a long time to read and enjoy the Lord's word daily and to receive the Lord's word into you. This is like a person taking in food. Not only does he have to receive; he has to take the food into him. If you would allow the Lord's word to be digested in you, the digested word will become the living and instant word spoken out from within you when you go to the meeting. Paul told the Hebrew believers, "For when because of the time you ought to be teachers, you have need again for someone to teach you what are the rudiments of the beginning of the oracles of God, and have become those who have need of milk and not of solid food....But solid food is for the mature, who because of practice have their faculties exercised for discriminating between both good and evil" (Heb. 5:12, 14). This shows us that the mature ones who can take in solid food have had their faculties exercised through practice. This is why you must be exercised in the Lord's word.

To be exercised in the Lord's word means that you do not just receive the Lord's word; you also allow the Lord's word to be applied in you and in your daily life. In other words, you must apply the verses that you pray-read and memorize every morning to your practical daily living. The more you apply them, the more they will be used. The more they are used, the more you are exercised. The more you are exercised, the more you become skillful and well trained. Suppose this morning you read 1 John 2:15, "Do not love the world." You should apply this in your living today. You should pray, "Lord, You love me. You have redeemed me. Now I belong to You. I love You. I do not want to love the world." If you pray this way, you will touch the Lord and the Lord's word will operate within you. When you go to the department store to shop and pick up an item, something within will say, "Do not love the world." When you drop it and you pick up another item, something within will say again, "Do not love the world." If you drop that and pick up a third item, something within will say, "This is the world." In the end, you will not buy anything. This is how you apply the word "Do not love the world" in your practical living.

This kind of experience will enable you to speak the living word. When you open up your mouth to speak in the meeting, your speaking will not be merely letters from the printed Bible; rather, it will be words that you have digested and experienced. We should speak this kind of word in the meeting. While you are being trained here, you should not merely learn a technique for speaking. We previously mentioned different ways of speaking such as speaking with the word, with the Spirit, with singing, and with prayer. All these are necessary, but the person is the most important. You must take in and digest the Lord's word and apply it in your practical living so that the function of the Lord's word can be fully manifested in you. Otherwise, merely learning a technique will not work. If you merely use a technique, your speaking will not be living or practical but will be empty doctrines. Hence, you must practice. I hope that you will not practice merely memorizing two verses a day. That is for the other brothers and sisters in general. You who are burdened to serve the Lord full time for the rest of your life should labor in the

Lord's word to receive, take in, digest, be exercised in, and apply the Lord's word. In the end, your whole being will become the word. Today, I am advanced in age. For me to memorize the Bible chapter by chapter and book by book is not easy any more. But all the words of the Bible are in me. I am very clear where each verse is, and what each chapter talks about. This is why it is very easy for me to speak the Lord's word. I hope that you can be the same as I am. In the next few years, not only do you have to carry out the new way in Taipei; you must succeed in learning the Lord's word. In this way, no matter where you go in the future, you will be a person who takes in the Lord's word in a full way and is exercised by it.

A message given by Brother Witness Lee in Taipei on November 26, 1987.

CHAPTER TWENTY-THREE

LIVING IN THE SPIRIT TO CARRY OUT THE OVERCOMING WAY

In the past messages I have already pointed out that the proper way to meet and to serve as required in the Bible is an overcoming way by living in the spirit.

THE GOAL OF SOWING BEING FRUIT-BEARING

The goal in the Bible is that we live in the spirit to be a fruit-bearer. This can be seen clearly from the Lord Jesus' parable of the sower in Matthew 13:3-8. He said that a sower went forth to sow, and the seeds fell into four different kinds of soil. The first kind was the wayside, where the birds came and devoured the seeds. This indicates that when anyone hears the word of the Lord's gospel but does not understand it, the evil one comes and snatches away that which has been sown in his heart so that he cannot be saved. The second kind was the rocky places without much earth. The seeds sprang up immediately because they did not have depth of earth. When the sun rose, they were scorched; and because they had no root, they were dried up. This shows a person who hears the Lord's word, receives it, and is regenerated by it, but because of hidden sin and unexposed self within him, the Lord's word is not able to take root and grow in him. When affliction, trial, or persecution occurs, he is immediately stumbled, and his Christian life is finished. Hence, in this case there is no need to mention fruit-bearing.

The third kind was the thorny ground. When the thorns came up, they choked the seedlings. This shows a person who is not only regenerated and saved but who has also had this life grow in him. However, because of the anxiety of the age and the deceitfulness of riches, the word of life is choked, and it becomes unfruitful. Thus, he cannot be a fruitful citizen in God's kingdom. His Christian life also can be considered a failure. Although the seed of God grows in him, at the same time there are things from Satan, such as the anxiety of this age, the deceitfulness of riches, and various lusts, that compete with the seed of life God has sown. In the end, he fails. This does not mean that he is not saved or that he will lose eternal life and perish. Rather, it means that he has not attained the goal of fruit-bearing. Fruit-bearing is the goal in the Lord's parable of the sower. This indicates that a person not only must be saved and regenerated; he must also grow in life to bear fruit, at least thirtyfold. If he bears more, he will bear sixtyfold. The best is a hundredfold. This is represented by the fourth kind of soil, the good earth. It speaks of those who hear the word, understand, and produce fruit.

Here we see clearly that Christians are generally of four categories. The first category is those who are Christians in name, or who are on the edge of Christianity. Although they have heard the word, they have not believed and are not saved. Therefore, they have nothing to do with the fruit-bearing of life. The second category is composed of saved and regenerated believers. They have received the life of God, but they have not allowed this life to grow. The third category also is composed of saved and regenerated believers. They have some growth in the life of God. They even struggle and strive to bear fruit, yet they fail. The fourth category is the believers who bear much fruit in the Lord. They are what we call the overcomers.

ON THE BATTLEFIELD AND IN THE RACE

Today we are all in the Lord's recovery. We are not only the saved Christians, but we are also the meeting people. In which of the four categories of Christians should we consider ourselves to be? You must realize that the Christian's spiritual life is for both a battle and a race. Therefore, at the end of his life, Paul said, "I have fought the good fight, I have finished the course" (2 Tim. 4:7). Obviously, this matter was very important to him in his Christian life. But today, the spiritual living of many Christians is neither a race nor a battle; they spend their time foolishly and ignorantly. Although we are in the Lord's recovery, we should not be complacent. We should not make the Lord's recovery our hiding place. In the same token, what is set before us is a race, a battle. Although many of you are young, from the time you were saved and began to pursue the Lord, you have had the sensation that the Christian life is a battle and a race. Hence, I would repeat that the way of meeting and serving as revealed in the Bible is a battle and a race. We must take such an attitude, daily putting ourselves on the battlefield and in the race.

BEING SOBER, BEING WATCHFUL, AND LOSING THE SOUL-LIFE

For the above reason, in the New Testament, beginning from the Gospels, the Lord Jesus told His disciples again and again to be watchful, to watch and pray (Matt. 24:42; 25:13; 26:38, 41; Luke 21:36). In the Epistles, the apostles also taught us many times to be watchful and to be sober (Eph. 6:18; Col. 4:2; 1 Thes. 5:6, 8; 1 Pet. 5:8; Rev. 3:2). Today we are on the battlefield, not on a bed. When a man is on a bed, he can relax in every way. But when he is on the battlefield, he has to be on the alert all the time and be aware of everything going on around him. The Lord's recovery has been among us for over sixty years. From 1922 to 1937, within a period of a little over ten years, we realized that our way of meeting and serving was not up to the standard of the truth of the Bible and that there was the need for change. By 1984, I saw the degenerating condition among us; many saints were half asleep. I was very depressed within. At that time I knew that this kind of situation could not be solved by merely holding a few conferences. Something had to be done from the root. This time we should afford the Lord an opportunity to move on among us, something we have been unable to do in the last few decades.

The first item we began to practice was gospel preaching by door knocking. I believe all you trainees have tasted the joy, the song, as well as the tears in this matter. The tastes of sourness, sweetness, bitterness, and spicy hotness are all there. If you want to be an overcomer by visiting people for the preaching of the gospel, you must be prepared like an athlete in the Olympic games. During the time of the competition, every aspect of your life has to be adjusted and restricted. You cannot eat as you please, and you cannot do as you please. This is a suffering. It causes you to lose your soul-life. This is why the Lord said repeatedly in the Gospels that man has to "lose his soul-life for My sake" (Matt. 10:39; 16:25; Mark 8:35; Luke 9:24). To lose the soul-life means to cause the soul to lose its enjoyment and to suffer. It is not too hard to knock on the door of our relatives and preach the gospel to them. But to knock on a stranger's door is not easy. For that you have to lose your soul-life. Therefore, before you go out to knock on doors, you have to spend at least twenty minutes to deal with sins, to pray, and to be filled with the Holy Spirit. These three items are the prerequisites for our going out to knock on doors. Anyone going out to knock on doors without dealing with sins, praying, and being filled with the Holy Spirit will definitely make the trip in vain. But if you spend twenty or thirty minutes to deal with sins, to pray, and to be filled with the Holy Spirit before going out to knock on doors, your preaching of the gospel will be victorious, and you will experience in a genuine way that the Lord is one with you and that His power and authority are with you.

BUILDING UP OUR FAMILY TRADITION
OF DOOR KNOCKING

Although I have been a Christian for sixty years, I have just discovered that to preach the gospel in an absolutely overcoming way, we must knock on doors. Today the most universal and effective way to preach the gospel is by door knocking. During the last year and a half in which we practiced door knocking here, we baptized over thirty thousand people. No other method can compare with this. Also, its advantages are many-sided. Our former way of preaching the gospel reached only the ones that we were acquainted with; but when we practice preaching the gospel by door knocking, we contact many that we did not know and could not reach before. Because of this way of door knocking by sweeping through a district, house by house, we have not only gained thirty thousand new ones, but, unexpectedly, have also recovered over two thousand dormant brothers and sisters.

Previously I gave you a budget. If one fourth of the saints meeting with us would go out to knock on doors, in just thirteen years, by the year 2000 A.D., all the doors in the whole world would be knocked on by us. Today, the gospel has been preached in every corner of the world; but it has not reached every household. In order to send it to every household, there must be the door knocking. We have discovered that no other way of gospel preaching requires us to pay a higher price than door knocking. Door knocking requires that we sacrifice our time, our family life, our face, and our self. This is just as the Lord told us, "I send you forth as sheep in the midst of wolves" (Matt. 10:16). However, He also said, "a son of peace is there" (Luke 10:6). Our Lord knows that among the wolves there are still the sheep, the sons of peace, and He wants us to go and bring them out.

From now on, in the Lord's recovery, we must lead the church to practice this matter of door knocking for the preaching of the gospel. This does not mean that we take door knocking as a condition for the receiving of a saint. We cannot expect every saint to preach the gospel by knocking on doors. But we do hope to build up this family tradition of door knocking among us. Today in Taiwan, both knowledge and riches are abounding. Entertainments of all sorts also have increased. If we still use the old way in gospel preaching, we will not succeed. We must pay the price to be an overcomer, to take this overcoming way to preach the gospel by knocking on doors.

PAYING THE PRICE TO BE AN OVERCOMER

Our door knocking to save people is just the first step. In the next step we need to care for the new ones we have gained. This also requires us to be overcomers. Although our present way of carrying out the home meetings, group meetings, and district meetings is still under study, as a whole it has been settled. I believe you have experienced this one thing, that is, if you are not an overcomer, if you would not live absolutely in the spirit, put aside the world, and deny the self, it will be difficult to take care of a home meeting or a group meeting. You can still go to the meeting, but you will be cold and dead, having nothing to supply to others. At most, you can help people learn some doctrines. You must remember that the biblical way, whether for meeting, gospel preaching, or serving, requires that we be overcomers. When the Lord Jesus sent the seventy disciples two by two to visit all the cities, He told them clearly that He sent them as lambs in the midst of wolves (Luke 10:1-3). No one knew what danger awaited them. But the disciples had no excuse. They had to overcome. Since we want to follow the Lord, we must overcome in everything. To preach the gospel and to take care of home meetings and group meetings all require us to overcome. If we do not overcome, we can do nothing.

I encourage you to exert your best effort to study the Bible and to pursue the truth. But these are only tools. Basically, you must be a right person. You must have fellowship with the Lord; you must have nothing between you and the Lord. Your conscience must be without condemnation, and you must not have any offense toward man or God. You must be a person who lives in the spirit. You must be such a person now, not waiting until the future. The Bible tells us that if man wants to receive salvation, he can do it now; there is no need to wait. In the same way, if you want to overcome, you can do it now. If you want to be filled with the Spirit, you can be filled today. This is absolutely possible. Perhaps in an hour and a half you have to go to take care of a meeting, but yesterday you lost your temper with someone. You can confess right away and ask for the Lord's forgiveness. You can pray, "O Lord, be merciful to me. I am going to the home meeting now. Fill me. You must go with me. Lord, I am a pitiful man. A person such as I can still serve You.

Lord, forgive me." After you pray and confess in this way, go to the home meeting. The Holy Spirit will surely fill you.

LEARNING THE TRUTH AND HAVING THE EXPERIENCE

I heard that when you go to the home meetings, some homes welcome you very much. They invite you not only for tea but also for meals. Of course, this is very good, but you cannot depend merely on others' welcome. Even if some homes do not welcome you but give you long faces, you still have to go. What you can do is based on the price you pay. The price you pay will determine how much you will overcome before the Lord. The price that you pay is your capital; the truth that you have learned is just your means or channel. Of course, if we have not learned the truth, even if we pay the price to be overcomers, it will not be possible for us to have the utterance because of the lack of the word. We must have the truth as the channel, and we must pay the price to dispense into people what we have experienced. As a result, what we give to others will not be merely teachings of truth, but what we have learned, experienced, and obtained from the Lord.

When you go to take care of the home meetings, someone may advise you out of a good heart, saying, "You are so young and are quite smart. Why don't you go back to school or go abroad to get a higher degree? Or why don't you start a business? This way of running around every day without accomplishing anything or gaining a name for yourself is too great a sacrifice." At this time, based on your own experience, you can say to him, "Brother, thank you for your kind concern. When Mary poured out the precious ointment on the Lord Jesus, some complained, 'Why this waste?' Throughout the ages there have been countless people who poured out their precious lives as ointment on the Lord. To the world, this is a waste. But I am willing to waste myself for His sake!" He may not understand your word, but the Holy Spirit will work in him, and your word will be deeply impressed into him. The spirit and attitude of your speaking will be planted in him like a seed. There is no need to persuade him to consecrate or sacrifice himself. Something will have been wrought into him already.

LIVING AN OVERCOMING LIFE DAILY

We who serve the Lord can exhort others to love the Lord, to be spiritual, to study the Bible, to pray, to deny the self, and to reject the flesh, but what is important is whether we ourselves have these experiences, and whether we are such persons. Especially you full-time trainees, you who have given up everything to be for the Lord, should be ones who fellowship with the Lord every day, dealing with Him, living according to the spirit, and having genuine experiences in your daily lives. When you come to the meetings, whether large or small, spontaneously you will be able to release something from within. With either a long message or just a few sentences, you will be able to supply others with what you have received and experienced. This is the meeting that the Bible talks about. Probably, not every saint in the meeting can do this. The church is like a home. There are the old, the young, the sick, and the lame. But I hope that at least one-tenth of those meeting with you can do this. I hope that all the trainees will be such overcomers, not only during the training period but also in the future, wherever you may go. While you are in the training, you should build up such a life. After the training, whether you return to school or to a job, do not forget the training that you have received here but continue to live this kind of life. You are different from others. You are those who live in the spirit. Wherever you meet, you will be able to function properly. Thus, the Lord will have a way to go on.

I hope every one of you can see clearly that you are being trained here not just in methods of the new way: knowing how to preach the gospel or to take care of the home meetings or group meetings. All these are less important; they are not our main emphasis. Our main concern is whether or not we are living in the spirit and living the overcoming life. For this kind of life, first, there is the need to pay a price and to sacrifice oneself to go out regularly according to a schedule to preach the gospel by knocking on doors, to bring people to salvation and reap fruit yearly. I hope that you all are the fourth kind of soil, which is the good earth, growing in life and bearing fruit abundantly. However, you should not despise those who would not do this, and you should not be concerned with those who criticize you. You yourselves must have the determination before the Lord that you will bear fruit in season. Second, you must live in the Lord's presence and speak the Lord's word to people every day. Third, in any meeting, you must follow the Spirit of the Lord to release the riches that you have experienced, realized, and obtained. I hope that all the churches will practice this overcoming way and bring the brothers and sisters into this overcoming way.

A message given by Brother Witness Lee in Taipei on December 1, 1987.

CHAPTER TWENTY-FOUR

BEING A MAN WITH A VISION

Scripture Reading: Acts 26:18-19; Phil. 3:13-14; 2 Tim. 4:7-8

THE VISION OF THE LORD BEING AMONG US

Since 1984 when I returned to Taipei, I have been very clear that the Lord's changing of the system must start from Taiwan. If the Lord's recovery is without such a change, and if there are no full-timers raised up, there will gradually be no way to go on. The way of Christianity eventually leads to a dead end. For this reason, the Lord raised up His recovery among us. We have to admit that we have had our shortcomings and weaknesses in the past sixty plus years. We have fallen short and become loose. But there is a fact, which even those who disagree with us or oppose us cannot deny, that in the Far East, and especially among the Chinese-speaking Christians, we bear a great influence. In many things they follow us to improve, but their rate of improvement is very slow because they do not have an absolute heart. This is one difficulty that exists.

Such a difficulty has occurred again and again in history. For example, during the time of the Reformation by Luther, the Roman Catholic Church had been in existence for about a thousand years. One can imagine the greatness of her power and influence. Had it not been for what Luther saw, and for his courage and boldness, he would never have dared to rise up to initiate the Reformation. Those who were closer to Luther were more faithful; and those who were farther away were less faithful. Gradually, the farther they moved away, the less absolute they became. Throughout the ages, the Lord's way on this earth has always encountered such difficulties. Although many may say that they are in the Lord's recovery, the degree is quite different. Today, whether Christianity likes to hear it or not, I have to speak again and again concerning the vision I have seen. I have been speaking on this vision for over fifty years. I am not stubborn, nor am I proud. But I have to declare to the universe that I am a person who has seen the vision. I must admit that I am chosen by the Lord; I am called by the Lord.

BEING FAITHFUL TO THE END IN FOLLOWING THE VISION

Due to the Lord's sovereignty, I was born into Christianity. Even though I had not yet been saved, I defended Christianity quite often. One day, a young lady preacher came to our hometown to preach the gospel. Out of curiosity I went to listen. I heard her speak, based on the story of Pharaoh's ruling, dominating, and enslaving the children of Israel, that the whole world was under the domination of Satan and men became his slaves to serve him. At that time, the Lord caught me with this word. I was deeply moved. Spontaneously I had a longing and a deep sensation that henceforth I should not be under Satan's enslaving any longer. When I walked out of that big chapel, I remember clearly that on the way home, I lifted my head and looked toward the heavens and said in my heart, "O God, even if the whole world were offered to me, I would not want it. From this day on, I just want You. I would be a poor preacher carrying my Bible bag and preaching the gospel from village to village for You."

From that day on, my whole being was changed completely. I gave up all my past desires and pursuits. I was only interested in studying the Bible. Very quickly, I finished reading through the whole Old and New Testament once. Later, I heard that there was a place that had the most excellent Bible exposition, a meeting of the Brethren assembly. I went to join them. Because I had just been saved and knew practically nothing, I was immediately attracted by them. Daily I loved to study the Bible and listen to expositions on it. After seven years, the Lord showed me clearly the way of the recovery. I then determined to leave that place, and began to cooperate with the Lord and be used by Him. By 1932, a church was raised up in my hometown, Chefoo. That was the first church in northern China raised up in the Lord's recovery. From that time until now, for 55 years, I have never changed the tone in my speaking. If I could liken the church in the Lord's recovery to a ship and myself to a pilot, I can say that I have never given up my compass, neither have I changed my direction. However, during this period, I have seen many wavering and staggering in this way of the recovery, some even wandering hesitantly along the border.

In 1949, I began to speak for the Lord in Taipei. Today it has already been thirty-eight years. You have never heard me change my tone. This does not mean that I have never gone through any storm. On the contrary, the more fierce the storm is, the clearer my direction is. From the first day that we began our work here, we made the decision not to touch Christianity, but to concentrate on the preaching of the gospel, bringing people to be saved, to love the Lord, and to grow in life and in truth. We had a good beginning here. Within a short period of six years, a great revival was brought in. At that time, the brothers desired to seek spirituality. They invited an outsider to visit us. This caused a big problem among us. Later, I was forced to release thirty-six messages concerning the matter of the church. All those messages were put into a book entitled *The Testimony and the Ground of the Church*. Because of this, the truth was further established and brought to light. In 1962, I began to work in the United States. For the last twenty years, I have also seen many being unsteady and uncertain. But I have always remained the same. The reason for this is that I have had a clear vision within.

A MAN WITH A VISION

We know that Paul was originally a stout defender of Judaism. He inherited the tradition from his fathers and was excessively zealous for religion, trying his best to persecute and ravage the church of God. One day, while he was on his way to Damascus to bind all those who called on the name of the Lord, the Lord met him and spoke to him, "Saul, Saul, why are you persecuting Me?" He said, "Who are You, Lord?" The Lord answered, "I am Jesus, whom you are persecuting" (Acts 9:1-5). This was the gospel that Paul heard and the vision that he saw. This "Jesus" was no longer individual; rather, He was corporate. He included Stephen, and all those who believed in Him. They were a part of Him. Whoever persecuted Stephen persecuted Him. To persecute the Christians was to persecute Jesus.

This Jesus is the Jehovah who created the heavens and the earth. He is the Triune God. One day, He became flesh. He lived on the earth for thirty-three and a half years as a man. Ultimately He went to the cross to die for our sins. He terminated the old man, the flesh, Satan, and the world. Then He was buried, entered into Hades, passed through death, was resurrected from the dead, and became the all-inclusive life-giving Spirit. Today, this Jesus is joined as one with Peter, James, John, Stephen, and thousands of those who believe in Him. He has become a great, universal Jesus. Hence, the gospel that Paul heard from the first day was a gospel concerning the mystery in God's economy. This gospel became his vision.

Later, the Lord told him, "Rise up and enter into the city, and it shall be told you what you must do" (Acts 9:6). This is the second part of the gospel that Paul heard: This Jesus who was revealed to him had a mysterious Body, which was composed of many members. Now the Lord would not tell him directly what he should do; rather, He sent a member of His Body, Ananias, to initiate him into the union with this Body. Although Paul could not see anything physically at that time, he was clear within. Formerly he was leading others; now he was led by others. Ananias laid his hands on him so that he might see. Ananias then baptized Paul and charged him to call on the name of the Lord that he might wash away his sins. This was the vision that Paul saw: Jesus, Ananias, and the words which they spoke. Moreover, this vision included the way that he walked the rest of his life, as recorded in Acts 26:17b-18: "To whom [the people of Israel and the Gentiles] I [the Lord] send you, to open their eyes, to turn them from darkness to light and from the authority of Satan to God, that they may receive forgiveness of sins and an inheritance among those who have been sanctified by faith in Me." From that day on, what Paul preached and worked was fully controlled by the vision he saw; he never deviated from it. This is why he could testify before the king saying, "Wherefore, King Agrippa, I was not disobedient to the heavenly vision" (Acts 26:19).

NOT FORSAKING OUR INHERITANCE

The inheritance we have obtained is not a heavenly mansion, or any creature in the universe, but the very Triune God Himself. Not only has He become our life, He is even our possession. He is the inheritance which we have received, just like a portion of the good land that was allotted to each Israelite in the Old Testament. When we were saved, we received the Triune God to be our Savior. This is the first part of our inheritance. The second part is the Triune God as our life. Since we have received this inheritance today, we should do our best to enjoy it. Paul said in Philippians 3:13-14: "But one thing—forgetting the things which are behind and stretching forward to the things which are before, I pursue toward the goal for the prize of the high calling of God in Christ Jesus." The prize here is the inheritance. Our enjoying of the inheritance is our gaining of the prize. Today, we all have been saved and regenerated. As long as we are running the course before us by the salvation and life we have received, and properly enjoy the inheritance given to us by God, we will be able to enter into the kingdom to partake of a greater and richer inheritance when the Lord comes. Otherwise, we will lose our prize and will have no part in the coming kingdom; we will be punished and cast into the outer darkness.

When I was raised up by the Lord to give up my job to serve the Lord full time, many came to discourage me. The first ones were my in-laws. They entreated me saying that it was all right for me to believe in Jesus or even to preach, but why did I have to give up my profession? At that time I had a very good job. They wanted me to seriously reconsider. Then when my schoolmates heard that I was going to be a poor preacher, they thought that I was crazy. All of them came to rebuke me for being so foolish as to choose a way that men despised. In spite of all of these, the vision within me was very clear. I knew that I had received the inheritance of God and that I could not forsake this inheritance. From that day on, by the Lord's grace and mercy, I have been enjoying this inheritance every day.

ENJOYING THE TRIUNE GOD
AS OUR SUPPLY, PRIZE, AND ETERNAL PORTION

God's inheritance is our enjoyment today. The continuation of our enjoyment today will become our enjoyment in the kingdom for the future. The enjoyment in the kingdom will further develop into the enjoyment in the new heaven and the new earth. Our enjoyment of this inheritance in the kingdom is the prize of God's high calling. Paul was such a person who had received the prize. In Philippians 3 he said, "Not that I have already obtained or am already perfected, but I pursue" (v. 12). This means that although he had received quite an inheritance, he still had not fully obtained it. That was why there was the need of "forgetting the things which are behind and stretching forward to the things which are before, I pursue toward the goal" (vv. 13-14). Not only had he forgotten all the things which he had before in Judaism, but he also laid aside all the inheritance that he enjoyed in the past, to pursue after the coming inheritance. At the end he finished his course. It was not until he was about to be martyred that he was confident of the kingdom prize. He testified to his young co-worker Timothy, "I have finished the course ...henceforth, there is laid up for me the crown of righteousness, which the Lord, the righteous Judge, will award to me in that day; and not only to me, but also to all those who have loved His appearing" (2 Tim. 4:7-8).

We have seen that the inheritance we received is the

Triune God. He is all the supply that we enjoy today, the prize which we will receive in the coming kingdom, and the eternal portion that we will enjoy in the new heaven and new earth. I have spoken very clearly for the last ten or twenty years concerning this matter. I have given you message after message on this subject. I would say that this has become my "shop-talk." Whatever I speak from this angle or from that angle is on this matter. This thing has filled me up. It has become my blood and my cells. My whole being is just this one thing. There are many aspects of this Triune God. Therefore the New Testament uses a great term, economy, to convey the thought that the Triune God has a desire, an intention, a plan, and an arrangement. This is also His administration, management, government, operation, execution, and completion. This is the economy of the Triune God. This economy is altogether wrapped up with the dispensing of this Triune God.

UNDERSTANDING THE MEETING
AND GOSPEL PREACHING
IN GOD'S NEW TESTAMENT ECONOMY

First of all, this Triune God is a unique God. He has no beginning and no ending. No one created Him, and no one begat Him. He is self-existing and ever-existing. At the same time, this Triune God has the aspect of three. There is the aspect of the Father, the Son, and the Spirit. But this does not mean that He has three names. Rather this is one name of the one God. Matthew 28:19 says, "The name of the Father and of the Son and of the Holy Spirit." The name here is singular. This shows that the Father, the Son, and the Spirit are not three names but one. In order for this Triune God to enter into man to be one with man, He made a plan in eternity past. Then in time He came to create the heavens and the earth, and He also created man. He called man to follow Him and taught man how to serve Him. He gave the law and sent the prophets. He set up the priests and appointed kings. He did many things, but no one knew why He did them.

After four thousand years, He came to be flesh. He

entered into the womb of the virgin Mary and remained in her womb for nine months in accordance with the law of creation. After He was born, He grew up in a poor carpenter's home in the city of Nazareth. After thirty years, He came out to carry out His ministry. For three and a half years He went everywhere healing the sick, casting out demons, preaching the word, and calling out disciples. Eventually, He died on the cross, was buried, and resurrected to become the life-giving Spirit. This Spirit is the ultimate consummation of the all-inclusive Triune God. In this Spirit there is Jehovah, the Father, the Son, the Spirit, man, humanity and human living, with crucifixion, resurrection, and ascension. This One is the Spirit that is spoken of at the end of the Bible (Rev. 22:17). Moreover, this Spirit is also the word. The word and the Spirit are inseparable; the two are one. This is why in Romans 10 it says that Christ is the word and He is near you, in your mouth and in your heart (v. 8). Now all you need to do is believe in your heart and confess with your mouth and call "O Lord Jesus," and He, the Spirit, will enter into your spirit to be mingled with your spirit to become one spirit with you. When you have Him, you will have satisfaction and rest, and when He has you, He will be fully satisfied. He will become your Savior, life, and everything. You can call on Him, enjoy Him, and testify for Him all the time.

As such a saved person, naturally you need companions, and you need to meet together with all the believers. This is the church. The main item in the church is the meetings. When we come to meet, we should not bring in the worldly elements, neither should we bring in the practices of Christianity. We do not want the world, neither Christianity, nor our self. We come in the way of emptying ourselves of everything and being filled with Christ. Therefore, everyone of us enjoys Christ in our daily life, and we become persons filled with Christ. And when we come to the meetings, we cannot help but open our mouths to sing and pray. In this way, everyone will sing, pray, and speak. This singing, praying, and speaking will fill the meeting with the riches of Christ, and the meeting will become the exhibition of Christ. This is the way that we must take today. This is called the recovery. This is also what we mean by the change of the system. The change of the system is not a change of dead methods; rather, it is to recover the meeting which the Lord desires according to the Bible. When we come together, each one has a psalm, or a teaching, or a revelation, or a tongue, or an interpretation (1 Cor. 14:26). In this way Christ will be supplied and ministered mutually to one another.

In addition, in order to spread the gospel, we must go out to visit people by door knocking. However, this is not the condition for the receiving of the saints by the church nor is this an item of our basic faith. Today in the church, in the Lord's recovery, there must be such an item of gospel preaching by visiting people. But we are not requiring everyone to go out to do this. We have a budget, that among the brothers and sisters meeting in one locality, there should be one fourth that would go out regularly throughout the year to visit people to preach the gospel. For the church to gain people and for the gospel to go out, there is no other way as widespread and far-reaching as this. No one who has tasted this would say that this way is not good. The reports from all six continents constantly prove that this is the most excellent way. If we have never gone out to visit people to preach the gospel, we have not consecrated ourselves to the Lord in an absolute way. If we are absolute in our consecration, surely we will go out to visit people to preach the gospel. To go among the wolves to search out and to save the sons of peace is most pleasing to the Lord.

BEING A MAN OF VISION,
AND TAKING THE WAY OF RECOVERY

We must see a clear vision. First, as a Christian on the earth today, we must be a person who goes out to visit people to preach the gospel. Although we cannot do this every day, at least we should do this once a week. For us to do this is to testify to Satan that we are those who have consecrated ourselves fully to the Lord and to His gospel. We have to build up such a habit in the way we serve the Lord. Second, after we preach the gospel and baptize people into the Triune God, we have to supply them with more of the riches of Christ. We should not bring them the world or religion; nor should we bring them Christianity; rather, we should bring to them the life that is filled with the vision in which we live every day. If we can lay hold of these two things and practice them seriously, the Lord will then have a way.

For this we must return to the way of meeting and gospel preaching revealed in the Bible. This way will enable us to spread the gospel and will help the sinners to be easily saved. After a person is saved, he will be liberated in a kind of free atmosphere to develop the gift of life within him. This is a recovered way and is also a sure way. Since the Bible has thus charged, surely the Lord will accomplish it. Man is prone to take the simple and easy way. The uphill way is hard, and not many are willing to take it; the downhill way is easy, and many are happy to take it. Our training here is to help every saint to turn around from the downhill way to the uphill way. This is the vision that we see, and the recovery that the Lord desires. If we cannot carry this out in this generation, the Lord will do it with the next generation. He has been waiting for two thousand years. He can wait longer. He has said, "On this rock I will build My church, and the gates of Hades shall not prevail against it" (Matt. 16:18). This word will not fail. He will surely accomplish what He has said. His word will surely be fulfilled. The Lord will surely work out the mutuality in meeting as described by the Apostle Paul in 1 Corinthians 14:26 and Hebrews 10:25. I hope that, after hearing these words, you can all have a clear vision within that the way we are taking today is not directionless, and the training we are receiving is not aimless. When I see so many of you young ones being trained here, not only do I rejoice, but I also have the full assurance that the future of the Lord's recovery is full of hope. May the Lord bless everyone who has a desire to take this way, and may the Lord also use this way of recovery that is revealed in the Bible.

A message given by Brother Witness Lee in Taipei on December 3, 1987.